Young Writers 2005 Creative Writing
Competition For Secondary Schools

T·A·L·E·S·

From Nottinghamshire
Edited by Lynsey Hawkins

Disclaimer

Young Writers has maintained every effort
to publish stories that will not cause offence.

Any stories, events or activities relating to individuals
should be read as fictional pieces and not construed
as real-life character portrayal.

Young Writers

First published in Great Britain in 2005 by:
Young Writers
Remus House
Coltsfoot Drive
Peterborough
PE2 9JX
Telephone: 01733 890066
Website: www.youngwriters.co.uk

All Rights Reserved

© Copyright Contributors 2005

SB ISBN 1 84602 220 7

Foreword

Young Writers was established in 1991 and has been passionately devoted to the promotion of reading and writing in children and young adults ever since. The quest continues today. *Young Writers* remains as committed to engendering the fostering of burgeoning poetic and literary talent as ever.

This year, *Young Writers* are happy to present a dynamic and entertaining new selection of the best creative writing from a talented and diverse cross section of some of the most accomplished secondary school writers around. Entrants were presented with four inspirational and challenging themes.

'Myths And Legends' gave pupils the opportunity to adapt long-established tales from mythology (whether Greek, Roman, Arthurian or more conventional eg The Loch Ness Monster) to their own style.

'A Day In The Life Of ...' offered pupils the chance to depict twenty-four hours in the lives of literally anyone they could imagine. A hugely imaginative wealth of entries were received encompassing days in the lives of everyone from the top media celebrities to historical figures like Henry VIII or a typical soldier from the First World War.

Finally 'Short Stories', in contrast, offered no limit other than the author's own imagination while 'Hold The Front Page' provided the ideal opportunity to challenge the entrants' journalistic skills, asking them to provide a newspaper or magazine article on any subject of their choice.

T.A.L.E.S. From Nottinghamshire is ultimately a collection we feel sure you will love, featuring as it does the work of the best young authors writing today.

Contents

Becket RC Comprehensive School

Jack Ramsden (12)	1
Jessica Gibbs (13)	2
Rebecca Kiely (12)	3
Hannah Beska (13)	4
Adam Sunderland (12)	5
Sophie Waters (12)	6
Richard McArdle (13)	7
Ellyn Piper (13)	8
Nathan Page	9
Natalia Ventrella (12)	10
Dominic Shakh (12)	11
Tom Lawrence (12)	12
Marie Cope	13
Gareth Thomas (12)	14
Niall Gibbons	15
Siobhan Coffey (11)	16
Zac Parker (12)	17
Richard Horgan (12)	18
Huw Rees (12)	19
Tyler Dore (12)	20
Madeleine Kern (13)	21
James Ayland (13)	22
Navraj Padam (13)	23
Arun Lobo (11)	24
Imahn Josephs	25
Jack Stevenson (12)	26
Priya Vaseer (11)	28
Thomas Pegg (13)	29
Leo Dolan (13)	30
Joseph McArdle (13)	31
Poppy Miszczak (13)	32
Michael Bratt	33
Ciara Molloy (13)	34
Gabi Rozwadowska	35
Clare McKenzie (13)	36
Thomas Doar (12)	37
Luke O'Brien (11)	38

Henry Mellish Comprehensive School
- Marie Pearce (12) — 39
- Sharnie Towl (12) — 40
- Lisa-Marie Mckeown (12) — 41
- Hayleigh Walker-Randle (12) — 42
- Ashley Huggett (12) — 43
- Casey Wombwell (12) — 44
- Nyala Skerritt (13) — 45
- Joe Robinson (13) — 46
- Luke Brown (13) — 47
- Kimberley Gough (13) — 48
- Krissie Suban (12) — 49
- Danielle Strickson (12) — 50
- Michael Tyers (13) — 51
- Lee Read (11) — 52
- Nedean Betteridge (12) — 53
- Tiffany Colagiovanni (12) — 54
- Shirley Kutadzaushe (11) — 55
- Ashley Leighton (12) — 56
- Jessie Harrison (12) — 58
- Nikki Edwards (12) — 59
- Kayleigh Alicia Potter (16) — 60

Redhill Comprehensive School
- Rebecca Bancroft (12) — 61
- Laura Bray (12) — 62
- Sophie Macmillan (12) — 64
- Laura Harvey (11) — 66
- Siân Brooke (11) — 68
- Matt McAdam (12) — 70
- Hannah Spencer (11) — 72
- Bradley Nightingale (11) — 74
- Hannah Smith (12) — 75
- Siobhan Pannell (12) — 76
- David Saunders (12) — 78
- Nicholas Baxter (12) — 79
- Chelsea Mitchell (12) — 80
- Matt Gell (11) — 81
- Nicola Gretton (12) — 82
- Chloe Clapp (12) — 83
- Chris Bridgett (11) — 86

Anna Wakefield (12)	88
Amanda Ferguson (12)	89
Bethany Peace (12)	90
Narisha Lawson (12)	91
Luke Bailey-Jones (12)	92
Jonathan Bradley (12)	93
Becca Haynes (12)	94
Hayley Webster (11)	95
Dale Cross (12)	96
Emily Head (12)	98
Catherine Parr (12)	99
Michael Dawn (12)	100
Ellis Blower (12)	101
Gemma Senter (12)	102
Sarah Coulson (12)	103
Rosa Vince (12)	104
Rosa Spencer-Tansley (12)	106
James Mitchell (12)	107
Becky Payne (11)	108
Aimie Whitchurch (12)	109
Lewis Jeffries (11)	110
Atlas De Ville (11)	111
Harry Marshall (12)	112
Keila James (12)	114
Kimberley Morley (12)	116

Retford Oaks High School

Sam Geoghegan (13)	118
Jamie Lawrence (12)	119
Tom Newby (14)	120
Rebecca Newman (13)	121
Callum Harrison (12)	122
Sarah Chance (13)	123

The Wheldon School & Sports College

Matthew Baker (12)	124
Hayley Johnson (12)	125
Tammy Hart (11)	126
Peter Woodfine (12)	127
Emma Truman (11)	128
Hayley Brodsky (12)	130

Lynnette Sullings (12)	132
Rebecca Glynn-Matthews (12)	133
Elishia Khan (12)	134
Laura Brooks (12)	135
Hannah Batchford (12)	136
Georgia Binkley (12)	138
Jade Messom (11)	139
Amber Knight (12)	140
Tyler Lamb (11)	142
Kim Watson (12)	143
Emma-Louise Wilson (12)	144
Jacob Reeve (12)	146
Ashley Dennis (12)	147
Samuel Wiser (11)	148
Holly Townsend (12)	150
Hannah Dawson (12)	152
Laura Cooper (12)	154
Rebecca Oakey (12)	155
Stacey Vizard (12)	156
Ryan Campbell (12)	158
Stephanie Keating (12)	160
Ethan Ball (12)	162
Alexis Theobald (11)	163
Joe Reynolds (12)	164
Luke Ellis (12)	165
Melissa Brittle (12)	166
Sade Richards (12)	168
Hannaa Hamdache (11)	170
Danny Edwards (12)	171
Chloe Morris (11)	172
Tiffany Oakey (12)	173
Jordan Bedward (12)	174
Jade Bullock (12)	176
Gemma Rayner (12)	178
Piers Baird (11)	180
Grace Naghi (12)	181
Ben Naylor (12)	182
Lucy Savedra (12)	184
Carla Morris (12)	186
Abigail Hart (12)	188
Amy Hook (12)	189
Emma Glossop (11)	190

The Creative Writing

Enemy At The Gate

My heart beats steadily like a war drum, hypnotically driving me forward. Into battle I march, a soldier, that's all I'll ever be, all I'll ever live for. Taking orders is what I do. I never ask questions, my legs just march, my gun just shoots and people just die.

The dry smoke from the battlefield clogs my lungs and stings my eyes but I march on ignoring the blinding pain, banishing it from my mind and concentrating on the task in hand. I rub the soot from my binoculars and stare into the scratched-up lenses. My gaze falls upon the horizon and fear spreads through my body like a contagious disease nibbling away at the small ounce of courage left inside of me. I try to get a signal through my mangled radio but all I get out of it is the crackling voice of static laughing at me and what I have become. For what is a soldier without orders? He is nothing, as am I and I always will be until the end of my life. And as the enemy approach the gate I start to think, *how long will it be?*

Jack Ramsden (12)
Becket RC Comprehensive School

Hoody Ban

A local shopping market in Kent is planning to try and ban hoodies and caps. The people working on this are arguing that young people who wear hoodies and caps are intimidating to elderly people and young children.

We spoke to a person who works at the shopping market who wants to remain anonymous, this is exactly what he thinks, 'Young people who just mope around with their hoods over their caps just look like up-to-no good delinquents'.

On the other hand it is just a fashion. Most young people don't wear it because they're up to no good, they wear it because they like it. We asked a couple of young people just what they thought. One young boy said, 'Those people who say wearing hoodies and caps make us look bad don't know what they're on about. We don't wear them because we want to look bad. We wear them because they look cool'.

We also asked another boy who lives in Kent, where the scheme is going on; 'I love wearing my hoody and cap because it keeps me warm and at the same time as keeping my face dry from the rain and it blocks the sun'.

A similar trial, which has taken place at a different shopping centre, has already taken place and the number of customers has already increased. Other shopping markets are likely to implement these measures if these trials are successful.

More updates later this week!

Jessica Gibbs (13)
Becket RC Comprehensive School

Modern Myths And Legends
(The following story is based on a King Arthur story)

There I was kicking my precious football around, the one signed by Wayne Rooney. This cute little girl came in, sobbing her poor heart out. I asked her, 'What's wrong?'

'My rabbit,' she sobbed, 'she is caught in a trap.' She burst into a fresh load of tears.

I comforted her and said, 'Don't worry, I will help.'

She led the way into Sherwood Forest. I began to get nervous but followed her. Suddenly a gang of huge 18-year-olds surrounded me. The girl whispered, 'Sorry, they made me.' They grabbed me and pinned me to the ground. I felt the football being torn from my grasp and it was handed over to my archenemy, Stephanie.

She laughed at me.

'Now,' she cried with a cruel gleam in her eyes, 'this should cost a hundred quid at least.'

I glared at her.

'If you want to see your football again, you will have to bring me the object on this paper. Got it?'

'Yes, yes,' I spat.

Afterwards her ugly sister, who wore no make-up and had her hair scrunched up in an old net, offered me if I set her up with a date, then she would tell me what the object was.

My best friend offered to date her as I had a girlfriend. When she came all dressed up, she was beautiful. The object, she told me was just a rock.

I therefore got my football back and my best friend and her are still dating.

Rebecca Kiely (12)
Becket RC Comprehensive School

Untitled

Chad had texted his girlfriend sixty times. She hadn't texted him back. He wondered if she had 'dumped' him, but if she had, then he realised he would be the laughing stock of the school.

Suddenly, the phone rang it was his girlfriend's mum. She explained that Megara had been missing for hours. Chad began to worry. His pride and joy - gone? But where, how? He immediately began to watch the news. Three girls missing, same hair, same eye colour. Only one explanation for this ... Syclla!

At the bottom of the Creek Baci Syclla drained the young beauty and grace from young girls. The girls had to be similar in hair and eye and body. She had drained two already, waiting for the third was easy. Ever since the gods cursed her this is all she ever did.

Chad ran towards the creek. Then he saw Syclla. Her glossy skin, slithering into the muddy water. Quickly Chad dived into the creek, slowly he swam after her, grabbing her by the tail, pulling her to the surface. Syclla was temporarily paralysed but there wasn't much time left. Chad swam faster and faster until he found her, lying in the weeds, drained. But he realised what had happened. When Chad had paralysed Syclla he'd also killed Megara because she was Syclla.

Six weeks later

Chad's mum had lost all hope. Never would she see Chad again. Their bodies were found, in an old boat on Creek Baci, drained, dead.

Hannah Beska (13)
Becket RC Comprehensive School

Killed In Action

Boom! A mortar just landed feet away from me, erupting in a torrent of fire and sparks. Fire is all around me, being dampened by the never-ending rain, thundering like thousands of artillery shells. The mortar has deafened me, I can see my commanding officer shouting orders at me, but I hear nothing. Then I see the white chemical flash of a phosphorus grenade, for a few terrifying moments I am blinded, and then my vision returns and I see my commanding officer on the floor limp and lifeless, blood trickling down his forehead, surrounded by many other bodies.

I look up at the sky and it's painted with sparks and smoke from missiles fired, like a horrific fireworks display. My pounding heart is almost as loud as the explosions around me, I hop over the trench, firing and emptying out the clip in my gun, I throw a grenade, and a terrified scream is cut off for a deafening explosion.

For a few moments I think I might make it to the other side, where the prospect of reinforcements await. Then a flash of lightning illuminates everything, and all thoughts of reinforcements are lost, as I see every one of my comrades strewn over the floor, then I hear the ear-splitting chatter of machine-gun fire, for a moment I lose all feeling, all my senses disappear, then all goes dark.

Adam Sunderland (12)
Becket RC Comprehensive School

A Day In The Life Of Cameron Diaz

Monday 20th November

Dear Diary,
   Got up this morning, with a smile on my face. But as soon as I got up and looked out of my window, I could see photographers, already. I just want them to leave me alone once in a while. I needed to get something from the shop down the road. Having to get dressed in some baggy clothes and a hat. I really don't want to wear these kind of clothes, but if I don't, my face will be all over the newspaper or in magazines.
   I travel down the road, bodyguards 10 feet behind and in front. I get my milk, then nip to McDonald's. As soon as I walk out of the shop, flashes everywhere. Blinding me.
   I walked home fast. My bodyguard's now five feet behind and in front. Paparazzi following me. Finally, I was back home. I had to get my things, to get ready for my photo shoot, with Heat magazine. My agent came to pick me up. With darkened windows, thank God.
   My normal day had started. We arrived at the Heat centre at about twelve. Had a salad, because, as my agent and everyone else tells me, I have to keep my figure down.
   I got my make-up, hair and clothes done. Took a few shots, then had an interview. Got driven home and had a low carb dinner. It was about two in the morning, when I finally was in bed, and finished writing my diary.

Sophie Waters (12)
Becket RC Comprehensive School

A Day In The Life Of Spider-Man

I'm Spider-Man, a superhero. I'm responsible for the whole of New York City, risking my life for the safety of others.

Boom ... and then a cackle. It was Hobgoblin. His green, twisted face turned into a wicked smile. He flew towards me on his high-speed glider, throwing an exploding pumpkin at me as he did so. I executed a triple twisting backflip to avoid it. In a split second I swung round, crashing into Hobgoblin, sending him flying off his glider and crashing down onto the ground.

Suddenly, Hobgoblin appeared around the corner, his blue, muscular body, covered in beads of sweat, glinting in the sunlight. He let out an evil laugh. 'So you thought you could get rid of Hobgoblin that easily did you?' he cursed, throwing another pumpkin towards me.

I dodged and shot web at him, but he broke free. I wasn't going to beat Hobgoblin using my weapons, but I might be able to defeat him using his.

Another large pumpkin came flying towards me, but this time I caught it in my web. Swinging it round and round like a hammer thrower, I sent it flying into Hobgoblin causing him to crash back into a building. It exploded and fell on top of him.

A more eventful day than normal, I thought as I swung back home.

A stirring from the rubble and a hand shot out.

'I'll get you Spider-Man if it's the last thing I do ...'

Richard McArdle (13)
Becket RC Comprehensive School

Hold The Front Page

Is teenage fashion a problem?

Today, teenagers have a lot of style but problems have come up. Deputy Prime Minister John Prescott recently banned people from wearing hoodies at Bluewater shopping centre in Kent.

Members of the public think that it's a good idea to ban hoodies and caps. They are giving young people a bad image and scare young children and because they hide their faces youths look like they are up to something. On the other hand some people think that young people seem to express themselves in their clothes. After all it's only a hood and a cap so what's so scary about teenage fashion?

Pop stars and footballers wear hoodies. People don't think they are scary! Hoodies have been around for a couple of years now and so why has the problem suddenly occurred?

In my opinion hoodies should stay. If it's what people want to wear they should be allowed to do so. If hoodies are so scary why are they still being made? People are supposed to feel comfortable in what they wear. Fashion should be a freedom of choice.

Bluewater are the only people banning them, what if it gets to the rest of the UK? Hoodies cost a lot of money, if children are banned from wearing them, that's hundreds of pounds thrown away, then parents will start to complain.

It's also said swearing has been outlawed in Bluewater. Swearing is foul and it should be banned.

Ellyn Piper (13)
Becket RC Comprehensive School

Destroy Or Not Destroy?

He did not see it coming, but it still did. He decided to come off-course to Bespin. They crashed in the mountain grasslands of Earth. It took 48 hours to discover whether it was Bespin or not.

Their leader was dressed all in black like the Earthling Darth Vader. He even had a light-torch like him. He can chop through solid objects, such as Earthling titanium, even the strongest of things. It will kill even the most armoured of people.

Earthlings don't know their whereabouts but neither do I at this set moment. I'm not an alien or an Earthling but a Symboite.

Symboite - being or something of nowhere. It took several years to realise what I could do, like fly and travel through time.

Their leader has Snake-men soldiers to obey his every small request. So don't try to kill him, that's if you can find him. He will get his people to find him, if you bring the things needed to connect without outer space. They need an intercom receiver, outcom decoder, a satellite dish and a rocket ship (they already have that).

So if you do happen to be in the mountains make sure you have none of those things.

Now prepare to enter the mountain grassland of Earth, where she will learn her fate …

Nathan Page
Becket RC Comprehensive School

Unwanted Island

No one is wanted or happy on Unwanted Island there is only sadness and misery across the endless deserted land; fine white sand, rocks and very few plants swaying in the rare Australian breeze with the exasperating sun glowering over it.

Unwanted Island is an island for orphans who are not wanted anywhere else, who do not deserve to lead a good life, so they are sent there for a period of time or maybe even for life. But being on Unwanted Island is not even a punishment it is torture, cruel, ruthless, like a nightmare you will never wake out of even if you do eventually leave.

The constable sits, glowing with vanity pampering herself between the cool shading rocks. The carers watch over the endless dry land, which is not the best of jobs, giving orders every now and then. But things are not so easy going ...

As barren and desolate as Unwanted Island is, it does have company, a creature that you will never have heard of before and is rare even on Unwanted Island; but if you were to see one it would be the last thing you saw.

Always.

The pink-checked tarantula is a treacherous beast you would never wish to come across. Its sharp glare will seep into your eyes leaving you rooted to the spot not able to speak or move any part of your body. You will die within 30 seconds.

Always.

So if you were to come across a pink-checked tarantula there is nothing you can do about it, don't waste your time praying and whimpering. Just glare back and imagine it as a dream. It's not painful so there's no point crying.

Sometimes it's too late!

Natalia Ventrella (12)
Becket RC Comprehensive School

Between Two Trees - Opening

Only idiots would go to Wallaby County, the hottest and most stranded desert in the world. I was one of those idiots.

My friends and I couldn't have been thinking straight. We stood there and stared at the withered trees. We thought that we were the only vital thing there. There were no plants, no flowers, no grass and certainly no water. We should have turned when we had the chance. I pleaded with them to turn back. They wouldn't.

People said it used to be a cemetery. They heard it from people who had read this weird book. It was called *'Tree Ghost'*. I thought it was nonsense.

It was about a queen who was killed by her only son. He wanted to be king and the queen was only 56 years old. From then on her soul wandered the streets of Australia. Then she found Wallaby County. She brought the dead back to life and made them search for her son. When they caught him they tore his flesh apart and later he was buried between two trees.

If I were you I would take this hint and remember it. If you see an army wasp or a red bull, run. But if you see an orange-tongued frog, run faster! These creatures will shove their tongue down your throat until you choke. Then they will hop down it so you die in pain.

That night we camped out. It was dark, I was scared. An owl hooted. I was scared. Something or someone was outside our tent. I was scared.

Dominic Shakh (12)
Becket RC Comprehensive School

Only Time Will Tell

'Quick Elizabeth, it's coming. You're almost there. Come on!' But Elizabeth wasn't listening. It was as if she was possessed, just getting somewhere without a sense of speech or sound. She turned, looking how far the tracker was behind her. And that's when she fell.

Her leg was wedged under a root of the many oaks by the lake. I jumped from the safety of my tree and ran to help her. There was only one thing for it. I would have to saw off the sandal buckle with my knife. Then the wolf came near. Maybe if we kept still, the creature wouldn't find us.

Elizabeth got up and ran with renewed energy. It was a struggle to keep up. We clambered into my tree to see the wolf making a desperate attempt to jump up.

The animal suddenly stopped its frenzy, its ears sharp and still, as though it could hear the unheard ... then we heard it too. The sound came to us clearer than spring water ... galloping, galloping! Then silence. As if the horse were a ghost. We could see a black-gloved hand, holding the golden, engraved handle of a flintlock, aim and ... a sharp blast shattered the air, and the wolf lay dead at the foot of the tree. Bloodied roots seemed to shrivel as the sight of the vulgar animal's death.

The anonymous rider came forward, giving Elizabeth a strange look, as if he had met her before, in a different world, a different time. Then immediately, he galloped off.

Tom Lawrence (12)
Becket RC Comprehensive School

Birthright

Xathia never used to be evil, she used to be an archangel. Then something happened, no one knows what. Many wonderful things have happened around Xathia. Some good. Some not so good. But all wonderful.

She lives within the Norwegian mountains, they used to be a beautiful place with wild rabbits and hares skimming through the long grass happily. Foxes chased the rabbits lurking slyly behind the giant oak tree. That was then.

Now, the temperature has drastically decreased. The animals that used to live there have all died out. And those that didn't? They were killed by Xathia and her loyal zombie troop. Now all that grows here is weeds and hatred. Hatred, bitter and pure for mankind.

However one mountaineer still treks up that hill every year. All by themselves with no weapons of any kind. They trek right up to Xathia's stone and metal house on the very peak of the mountains. Why would anyone want to go up there? They don't. They have to.

It was decided long ago by the four, a council of elders, that it would be birthright to try and change Xathia.

That's where I come in …

Marie Cope
Becket RC Comprehensive School

Going For Gold

There's a huge volcano in Toronto, Canada. It hasn't erupted in over 60 years. Some people think it's extinct, although others think it can erupt at any time. When it last erupted, virtually all the people living in Toronto died.

Now all there is is a valley with a fast-flowing stream running through it. The river has shiny, shimmering golden nuggets, lurking at the bottom. One of those tiny golden nuggets could buy you the whole of Toronto.

The valley is abundant with creatures. Some are cute, like squirrels, deer and salmon. Others are not so cute, like the moose, the brown bears and the worst of all, Bigfoot. The not so cute animals stay at the top of the valley. Usually.

If you don't bother the moose, it won't bother you. Usually. Whereas, the brown bear might charge at you.

But as for Bigfoot, even if you don't go too near it or bother it, you may as well say your last few words, arrange which coffin you want when you die and invite people to your funeral. It will kill you. Definitely!

Gareth Thomas (12)
Becket RC Comprehensive School

At The Top Of The Mountain

So, here we are. Mountain Top Caravan Park. I stepped out of the car and gave my legs a good stretch; after all we had just been travelling for a day and a half. You see we were on holiday here in America, and had travelled over from England. I was here with my mum, Anne, my dad, Mike, and my baby sister, Molly, who was only two years old and, of course, there was me, Callum, and I'm eleven.

After I had stretched my legs I had a good look around. As I looked around, I saw a forest to my right. Next to that were the real reasons why we were here - the mountains. We were hoping to go skiing and from what we could see there was plenty of snow about. We all had our own skis and ski boots, except for Molly, who was just learning to ski, and this was her second time.

We were staying in a chalet, which was really nice. It had two floors with enough room for five people. Later that night we organised what we were going to do, although we were definitely going skiing. We were discussing it, when we stopped and all listened to the grey wolf howling at the moon and we saw two bald eagles flying home for the night. When I went to bed, I started to wonder what the next two weeks would bring.

Niall Gibbons
Becket RC Comprehensive School

The Long Journey Full Of Surprises

Is it? Isn't it? Was it? Will it? Will they? Won't they? Really? Are these all questions you will ask yourself as you read through these pages? Well, let's find out.

There is nothing in the African desert, just sand, a few dead trees, and bugs. But they're not your average bugs, they're pretty big! Deadly, and not too friendly to come across. In fact, they are terrifying.

If you come across *any* bugs, run as if your life depends on it, because it does.

If you run out of water you'll be dead in 2, maybe 3 days. Like I said earlier, there is *nothing*, not even water. It used to have a small water supply, but that dried up years ago, for no apparent reason. *Poof*, it just vanished into thin air.

It's a great place for 'team building'. As Jodie and Luke were about to find out. (It is a great place for team building because you are alone with your friends. You'll have to get on otherwise you can't survive.)

'Work together' they said. 'Team building' they said. Yeah, team building, that's right. Making, building, searching for things to help them survive.

Will they or won't they? Survive that is. Well, if you want to know the secret you will have to read on ...

No one told them where they were going, I don't even think the teachers really knew themselves! The pilot knew that it was a dry, barren wasteland and that there was no water.

They said it would be a surprise ... and it was!

Siobhan Coffey (11)
Becket RC Comprehensive School

Lost In The Jungle

Suddenly, Shawn Langston awoke. First he smelt it, then he saw it … *death*. He looked around, but found no survivors on the plane. He soon realised that he hadn't been asleep, he had been unconscious. He then knew that if he didn't find water soon he would not live for much longer.

He checked his pockets and noticed that his mobile was still working, but there was no reception. He knew he had to get to higher ground, but before he could get higher he had to pass through the jungle and the dangers that lay waiting inside it. He left the plane and set out for the jungle, surprisingly he never stopped except to check his mobile.

As the jungle came into view, he started to move a bit faster. Shawn wanted to reach the jungle before nightfall. He never reached the jungle because he hadn't noticed that although he wasn't high up enough to get a reception to call anyone, he was still on top of a mountain (which meant that the jungle was on a mountain).

He saw what he thought was a stream or a river, but in fact it was the top of an enormous waterfall. Shawn moved towards it but sadly, by the time he realised what it really was, it was too late, he had already fallen off the end of the mountain and luckily was now hanging from a small and thin branch.

He was afraid, his life started to flash before his eyes. He thought it was the end. He didn't know whether this was it or whether he was going to die or not …

Zac Parker (12)
Becket RC Comprehensive School

Story Opening

The scorching sun of America burned the floor beneath my feet as I walked off the bus to Camp Green Lake, even though I knew I shouldn't be there. The trouble was no one believed the truth. I walked to the doors as my feet slightly slipped on the soft grains of sand. I'll tell you how I came to Camp Green Lake.

My whole life I seemed to be in the wrong place at the wrong time. I was walking home when a pair of shoes fell from the sky and hit me on the head. I suddenly heard sirens and instantly ran in case there was danger near me. The sirens (as I heard them) got closer and closer until the police car screeched to a halt right in front of me.

They arrested me and took me back to my house (not knowing what I did wrong). Apparently, the shoes I'd stolen (but I hadn't) belonged to my favourite baseball player, Clyde Livingston. They had been donated to a home for homeless children.

In court, Clyde said, 'I don't know what kind of person steals from homeless children, he's no fan of mine.'

The judge gave me a choice - either go to prison or go to Camp Green Lake and I chose Camp Green Lake.

I arrived and entered through the front doors. I sat down and a man with long, thin sideburns bent down and got out two Cokes and said, 'You want one?'

I answered, 'Yes thanks.'

He slowly turned around and said, 'You think you're funny?' as he passed the Coke to the other adult (or worker). Then he said to me, 'You thirsty?'

I replied, 'Yes.'

He answered, 'Well you better get used to it 'cause you're going to be thirsty for the next 18 months!'

Richard Horgan (12)
Becket RC Comprehensive School

The Vagador Pass

The Vagador Pass. No human has passed through one side and come out the other. It separates the land of Migerdorrow from the rest of mankind. At the eastern side of the pass is a village, peaceful and quiet. It has persuaded many not to try. In fact, many of the people have not tried because of fear. Usually. On the other side of the pass is a vast, green and beautiful land. However, the unforgiving pass is dominated by gargantuan creatures, otherwise known as Hytordons.

Hytordons are forlorn, evil, unforgivable, killing creatures. They don't leave the pass. Except one time, one dreaded mistake, two hundred years ago, there was one man and one deed. He went hunting in the pass one afternoon. He killed a deer. Being quite proud, he dragged it home. However, when he got there, he had the dreaded feeling of being followed.

He lived in the city of Vagadoria, a prosperous, flourishing city in the land of Migerdorrow. A Hytordon had followed him. One Hytordon survived, one city demolished, about five hundred people killed. That incident is how the pass got its name. I cannot tell you what a Hytordon looks like. No one has had the courage to tell.

The Vagador pass has high, snowy, treacherous mountains. The land of Migerdorrow is filled with fear. Impassable mountains surround it. Vagador is the only way out. Hytordons are preventing our escape.

My wish to Migerdorrow is that some day, someone will make it through the long, ancient and doomed pass.

Huw Rees (12)
Becket RC Comprehensive School

The Lisbon Luxury Camp!

The so-called 'Lisbon Luxury Camp' is supposed to be fantastic, but there is one thing that is fairly scary and spooky about it and that is very strangely … *the animals!* The camp is set near a clean lake with a mountain a few metres from it. It is in Lisbon, in Portugal, where this great but apparently spooky camp is.

Aidan Costa, who lives in Portugal, loves camps and going to them with his father, Garcia Costa. One night at the dinner table, Aidan asked his dad if he could go to the 'Lisbon Luxury Camp'.

His father smoothly replied, 'Haven't you gone to enough camps this year, Son?'

Aidan just sat there sulkily chewing on his pork, while his dad was waiting for an answer. There seemed to be no way he was going to get one, so he just agreed and said, 'Yes, you can go if you really want to, but this is the last camp you're going to this year.'

Aidan jumped with excitement out of his seat, ran to his dad and hugged him tightly.

A week later, Aidan and Garcia were at the camp talking to their leader, Emerton.

Half an hour later, they set off for the first adventure through the forest, looking at the animals and taking photos, when suddenly a bear pounced on one of the campers. Emerton turned and shot the bear with a small tranquilliser just in time before the camper was the bear's lunch.

In the evening they reached their camp and told spooky stories before going into their tents. And as they got in their tents, a strike of lightning hit a tree. That tree fell directly on the camp and …

Tyler Dore (12)
Becket RC Comprehensive School

A Day In The Life Of Britney Spears

I wake up and my head aches. I guess it was the MTV Awards last night. I get up and I get a glass of water. I notice a bruise on my arm. 'Oh! Those stupid fans! Why can't they leave me alone?'

I have a look at Bit-Bit, my dog, and remember I need to get her food! I grab my joggers and my pink sweatshirt and make my way down to the grocery store; I enter it and pass the magazine aisle and a look of horror falls over my face. I see on Heat magazine they have zoomed in on a zit that appeared during the awards. I feel raged. I grab the dog food, pay for it and run out. At that minute a crowd of fans come and swamp me. I make a run for the toilets.

'Ow, this is really killing my thighs. I wish I didn't have this baby yet. I'm too young.' I get in my Porche and drive down to the only place that calms me down, the recording studio! I get there and after an hour or so, Kevin comes to pick me up for a drive-thru McDonald's and we go home.

I like being famous but sometimes it's a real drag. I have to be perfect all of the time in case there are reporters around every corner. I have to watch what I do and I have to do the right moves but they always seem some way to criticising me!

Madeleine Kern (13)
Becket RC Comprehensive School

Robin Hood

'Argh!' Robin Hood burst out of the window, spraying glass everywhere, with flames licking at his heels. With two bags in each hand, stuffed full of money, he dived round the corner just in time to avoid the ripple of gunfire scorching his tail.

'Great job, Robin,' Little John cried as he threw a second grenade into the building, just to make sure no one followed them.

Robin dumped the money into a polythene bag and then the pair of them slipped on their oxygen masks and dived into the water.

Meanwhile ...

'Robin Hood and Little John should be back any minute.'

There was the sound of splashing water and a door slammed open. Robin and Little John burst through.

'We've got them!' Robin cried as he poured out piles of money that almost covered the whole floor.

'Excellent!' Friar Tuck exclaimed. 'The prince will be furious we are so close to victory.'

Meanwhile at Prince John's HQ

'They got away, Sir,' the sheriff sighed.

'Whhhaaaat! They got away! How?' Prince John screamed.

'They took us by surprise, Sir. Planted a bomb in one of the air vents. We lost fourteen men.'

'Hmm, they think they can beat me that easily do they? Double the security, triple it, plant mines, do anything you want, just don't let them make a fool of me again ... !'

James Ayland (13)
Becket RC Comprehensive School

Robin Hood Series 1:
The Beginning Of A New Era

2030 - Iraq, bin Laden and the rest of his troops were planning to meet Saddam Hussain and his troops to make arrangements.

Choppers flew everywhere and landed on the roof of the glass building. Troops and army men came out of the choppers with guns. They slid down the roof and were no longer in sight. This glass building was in the middle of the desert and it belonged to Saddam Hussain, the most deadliest known terrorist throughout the world. Saddam showed no mercy to anyone and he was planning to do something big, very big, that would be remembered over the years. There was only one thing stopping him though, Robin Hood.

Sherwood Forest

Hood has just robbed and killed the sheriff of Nottingham.

'Another victory for me,' Robin said, congratulating himself.

Someone else was there though, watching him.

'I wonder what I should do now? Maybe I'll kill the king,' he said laughing. *'Argh!'*

Someone had just shot at him. Robin stood still as a figure approached him. It wore a black cloak and held a BB gun. He was from Iraq. He dropped a piece of paper in front of Robin and left …

Navraj Padam (13)
Becket RC Comprehensive School

Hanuman - The Monkey God

In India, a long time ago, there was a childless king called Dasaratha who longed to become a father, so he sacrificed one of his best horses and gave cakes to his three wives. The youngest, Kaikeyi, refused hers because she had been handed her cake last and a bird came and carried the cake away into the forest and dropped it. Vayu, the god of wind, blew it into a hand of a monkey named Anjana. She turned it around many times before a great god, Shiva, came down onto Earth and ordered her to consume it. She did so and soon Hanuman the monkey, son of Vayu, was born.

Hanuman inherited the powers of flight, shape-shifting, strength and invisibility from his father but he also inherited his appetite - a god's appetite. One day he saw the sun in the sky and, mistaking it for a golden fruit, he flew up to eat it. The sun fled but Hanuman chased it all the way to the heaven of another god - Indra. Indra saw Hanuman chasing the sun and he knocked Hanuman down to Earth with a mighty thunderbolt. Vayu saw this and went mad. He swept into the bodies of all the gods and tortured them with burning indigestion. Indra was forced to make peace with Vayu and Hanuman and he granted Hanuman the gift of immortality. Now immortal, he went on to help Prince Rama defeat the mighty demon, Ravana. But that's another story …

Arun Lobo (11)
Becket RC Comprehensive School

The Shock Of Horror

There I was in France; there were lovely plants and large fields. I came to France with my mother and father for a picnic. We especially came to see the mountains. My father and I really wanted to climb the mountains but my mother didn't want to. So my father and I went to get the harnesses, they were free and there was no ticket man.

However, as we were climbing the mountain, I noticed that my father's rope was becoming thinner, but I thought I was imagining it, so I carried on. When I looked back again, my father's rope was so thin, it made him start to dangle, but then it snapped … had I just seen what had happened? I climbed down the mountain as quickly as possible.

When I reached the ground, my mother was screaming. However, I unbuckled my harness and ran to my father.

My mother looked for help but wasn't successful, so we had to stay the night. I thought of an idea. I began to tug sticks off the plants and trees and made a huge sign saying *Help*, but would anyone see it?

After a while there was a helicopter. I waved my hands to them, but would they be able to help? The pilot glimpsed my father and knew how to help, so they came down and helped my father. We both went with him, but where were they going to take us?

Imahn Josephs
Becket RC Comprehensive School

Robin From Da Hood

Robin from da hood,
Who's just moved from da wood.
He is a good man
Wit his bling, bling tan.

Rob-in from the rich,
Is how he got famous which
He gives to the poor
Who don't ask for more.

He's got his crew,
Here is a few,
With Lil John
Who's got da bomb
50 Cent
From River Trent
And Snoop Dog from Ogg.

They saw a loaded gangster
Robin turned into a prankster
He snuck up from behind
And wasn't being kind
He robbed a 100-buck
And handed it to Friar Tuck.

And then for the getaway
I wish there was a better way
The Bentley broke down
In the middle of the town.

They gave the cash to the needy
Who felt quite queasy
So they would get better
And write him a letter
That was another good deed done
While havin' lots of fun.

While he's not on da job
He might be eating a chip cop
He arrives in da club
Getting drunk on Bub.

He's there with his gangsta mates
And all the rap greats
He's got a new car
So he won't be walking far.

Now you've heard of Robin from da wood
Who don't live in da wood
So don't be bad
Or you'll be sad.

Jack Stevenson (12)
Becket RC Comprehensive School

The Queen To Be

I knocked on the door with the big lion handle.

'Send the fairy in!' beamed the fairy queen of all the mountains to the door keeper.

The huge door creaked as I went in. The queen had chosen me from five other fairies.

The queen was old and always moody to anyone she met. If she wanted something she would get it exactly the way she wanted it. But now the queen was very ill and was to die any day soon, so she needed someone to become queen next.

'Now, Miss Topia, you have done well to get this far and you will take my place when I leave to go to Heaven …' the old woman spoke quietly in disappointment as she left her throne to congratulate me.

'I … erm … well … didn't expect that … I thought I was only working for you,' I replied nervously as she led me into a small room in a large barn where the animals lived.

'You will live here now and you are to obey my rules and do whatever I want you to do or you will suffer the consequences.'

The other fairies began laughing while I stood in the corner of my room wondering what she could do. Could she starve me or make me kiss her feet? As far as I knew I would try my best. Hopefully. I started whispering to myself, 'I can do this …'

But I was beginning to think I couldn't …

Priya Vaseer (11)
Becket RC Comprehensive School

The Man Who Howls

News Flash!

'Another horrific murder has taken place in Werewolf Village. With 12 murders in the last six months there is only one man who can save us.'

The next morning some of the villagers noticed a black horse and a dark figure racing to the village. Who was he? The villagers picked up poles and went to meet him. The dark figure in a long jacket, black hair and boots stood there. Von Trap had come to save them.

That evening Von Trap would head up to the known hideout of the wolf. The castle. He sat in the bar waiting. 1am, time for him to go. Putting on his hat he left. Von Trap saddled his horse Black Thunder and raced off to the castle.

He entered the castle just as the wolf was changing. In the hallways lay a naked man pulling and tearing away his flesh. Instead of blood there was fur. He loaded his gun with a silver bullet. The wolf heard him and charged. 'Argh!' The beast took a bite out of his arm. He shot the beast in the face. It lay lifeless on the floor.

Von Trap looked at his arm. It was full of fur. He was gripped with pain, he began to change. He was turning into the wolf. His face grew longer. His teeth sharper. He was becoming the werewolf. He was hungry. He smashed through the door to hunt for flesh. Warm, bloody flesh.

I must hunt ...

Thomas Pegg (13)
Becket RC Comprehensive School

Sea Food

James and Danielle decided to go out on their boat. After about three hours, the clouds started to get dark and the wind began to pick up. 'James, we better get gone,' said Danielle.

'Another 20 minutes, OK?'

Then a freak wave blew up and capsized the boat.

Danielle woke up and saw her surroundings. She was in a big bed in a brightly coloured room. Her clothes were over the back of a chair. 'Where am I? James! James! James!'

Then a lady walked in. 'Calm down, you're safe now, welcome to my palace … lunch will be served soon please get dressed and come to the main room.' Then she walked out the door.

Danielle quickly got changed and walked down the corridor to the dining room.

The first thing she noticed was the strange smell, then she noticed the two strange people. 'Hello, I'm Anne and this is George, welcome to our sea palace. We rescued you but your companion was not so lucky, he perished with the wave. Now for lunch, we're having turtle.'

'I can't eat this, I need to go and lie down.' She went back to her room and then to sleep.

Four hours later Danielle woke to the sound of sobbing. She walked down the corridor into the kitchen. There in the corner was James.

'Danielle, you have to get out of here, they're cannibals.'

Then a light turned on and George and Anne stood there, 'Won't you stay for dinner?'

Leo Dolan (13)
Becket RC Comprehensive School

The Mysterious Monster

I got back from my first day of work and, on the window, I saw some blood. I walked over, looked through and before me was a dead pigeon, its head separated from its body! It was disgusting, but I was tired and it was late so I went to bed. As soon as I was in bed I heard scratching on the window, like a fingernail on a blackboard. But then it stopped and I fell asleep.

The next day was a Saturday so I stayed at home. I was walking to the toilet, when I heard a noise from a room. I tried desperately to open the door, but it was jammed. Suddenly, I heard a scrambling of feet, a crash and a slam. Whatever it was, it had freaked me out and disappeared.

Later on, after returning from the shops, I made myself a coffee. It was dark outside but I was wide awake. Then I heard it, that same noise. I rushed into my bedroom; that was where it came from. But it was gone again. I stared out my wide-open window. Bright green eyes stared back. I blinked and they were gone!

I woke up in the morning and, out of the window, I saw a cat. That was it! It explained the noises, the pigeon, the eyes, everything.

I went downstairs for my breakfast. Oh my God! My doors were smashed off their hinges and on the wall was written, 'You will die'!

Joseph McArdle (13)
Becket RC Comprehensive School

Horror Story

As I walked down the creaky old corridor with nothing but my flickering candle, I felt a cold shiver trickle down my back, a tickling sensation like icy cold water. I turned around, and saw nothing dripping from the ceiling or drops on the floor. I saw a brightly coloured ball of light, I wasn't sure if this was real or my candle was deceiving me. My candle kept going out and coming back on. Something whispered behind me. It was a little girl's voice. A blue figure was coming towards me, it bellowed, 'Get out, you're not welcome, so leave us alone.'

I ran downstairs. I tried to open the door, it was stuck. I tried to prise it open with all my might. The voice was louder and closer, cold sweat dripped down my neck. I was frantically trying to open the door and looking for a way out. He shouted, 'You can run, but you can't hide.'

I ran to a window and was going to jump but it was too high. I decided to hide. My breaths were really heavy. It was hard to catch my breath. The man smashed a glass bottle in half and reached for the knife. He walked straight past me and walked back. He saw me! I tried to run but I was too slow, he got me right against the wall and threatened me with a knife and bottle. The little girl shouted, 'No Daddy! No!'

Poppy Miszczak (13)
Becket RC Comprehensive School

Hallowe'en Dream!

It was a week before Hallowe'en and Ben's father, Jack, a scientist, promised Ben he would make the coldest, most frightening night ever.

Day after day Jack was working on his machine to revive monsters from the dead and one day, a bolt of lightning hit the machine and revived *Dracula*. His bloody teeth were sharp and he had a black cloak. Another bolt of lightning struck the machine and revived *Frankenstein*. He was strong and huge and had hands like rocky, big boulders. Jack couldn't believe it and he was extremely happy to give his son a bloody, scary, happy Hallowe'en or a sad graveyard.

It was Hallowe'en and the monsters grew stronger and suddenly broke out of their cage. Ben was having a Hallowe'en party and a couple of friends had arrived - Mike and Ryan. Jack thought this time was great to make Ben's friends scared as they never have been before.

So Jack went downstairs to the cage to get the monsters but he went mental as he saw the cage open.

Ben's friends, Mike and Ryan, went to get a drink and Ryan said to the mysterious waiter, 'Can I have a drink please?'

The waiter replied, 'No way,' and charged at Ryan and launched his head right off, it was *Frankenstein!* Mike ran to the front door but there was a bat which evaporated into *Dracula,* got a knife and plunged it through his heart.

Ben ran to the kitchen and saw his friends, dead!

Michael Bratt
Becket RC Comprehensive School

My Horror Story

The bell rang and there was a stir in the school. Chairs scraped, teachers trying to shout the homework, the burst of sunlight as the doors opened to the afternoon.

I struggled to fit my sketchbook into my bag. I was thinking about getting a new bag, so I won't have this struggle every Friday afternoon. I left the art room to find that there was nobody around. I didn't think anything of it at the time, though maybe I should have. I left through the dark iron gates. I hated those gates with their sharp-pointed tips and its creak that reminded me of when my poor cat was run over.

I came to the edge of the road, which was so deadly quiet. I felt really uneasy. I stepped out onto the road and a car missed me by inches. As I stood there I couldn't help thinking, *where had the car come from?*

I carried on down the path trying my hardest to forget about the car, but something wasn't right about it. I turned just in time to see the same car whizzing towards me. I ran, not caring where I was going, just running.

After a while I chanced a glance behind me. I saw nothing. Was I imagining this car? I was relieved to see my house up ahead. I stopped dead in my tracks. There it was, I was sure now, but who was driving? I gasped, I recognised the driver, it was …

Ciara Molloy (13)
Becket RC Comprehensive School

The Lonely Walk Home

It was a Friday evening, for the first time ever I had to walk home alone. It was wintertime so it was dark, cold and stormy. I could see the lightning and hear the thunder roaring as if a wolf was playing the cymbals. The rain was becoming heavier, the wind was blowing and whistling. It was strange, I felt like I was being blown away. I could hear weird noises coming from a bush, but I didn't dare to look. I had so many thoughts going through my mind, none of which were positive.

As the bush was nearing, the fear inside me grew, was it a monster? Was it a wild animal or was it just a person? I didn't know. I looked around and there was no one there, I was alone, alone with nowhere to run. I knew I would have to face my fears and stand up to the mysterious creature.

My steps were getting smaller and shorter, they were getting slower. My heart was beating faster, more rapidly and I didn't know which way to turn, but there was only one way, forward to the strange noise. My umbrella was up, I thought it would act like a shield, thinking it would hide me from the creature, but it ripped and blew away. It was closer than ever. I knew that soon I would have to approach it. This was it, I turned to face …

Gabi Rozwadowska
Becket RC Comprehensive School

Swallow Song

The open window in Greg's room had caused no bother to him until now. The window was swollen and could not close. Every night a blackbird would land on his window sill and caw, then fly away again. Tonight however a slight wind was noticeable and the silk curtains were swaying to and fro gently around the window ledge. Greg waited till 10 o'clock, when the blackbird normally appeared. It wasn't until five to eleven when the swallow came. It was swooping around the tower, and the weathercock, and now it settled itself on the spot that the blackbird normally did, it began to sing the most beautiful song that Greg had ever heard.

Greg crept silently over to the window and listened to the beautiful bird sing. Greg was somehow hypnotised by the swallow, it seemed to be calling to him, swoop and dive. Greg must be as the swallow. Greg was just beginning to try and climb onto the window sill when the blackbird came. It cawed its usual caw. Three long caws and two short ones, like a fanfare, but the blackbird's normal song was a happy tune. However tonight the song had a mean tune to it, almost a murderous tune.

Greg still listened to the swallow's song: swoop and dive, swoop and dive and pushed the blackbird away and looking into the swallow's pure evil face, stood fully on the sill and leapt into the night.

Clare McKenzie (13)
Becket RC Comprehensive School

Robin Hood

There was a boy walking down the same street crossing at the same point to school as usual, his name was Ryan Hood. But today was not a boring walk to school.

He saw a lady on the other side of the road being robbed. They took her handbag. Ryan Hood chased the robbers. He was in the school's athletics team so he was quick.

After chasing them down the road, a car turned out of a side road and nearly hit the two robbers which made one of the robbers dive out of the way. (The one with the bag.) Ryan had caught up with them by then and he snatched the bag off the robber on the floor. Unfortunately the two robbers started chasing him, so Ryan started running but he thought, *instead of running anywhere I could run to school where there are lots of people.* Eventually he could see the school, after drawing nearer to the school the robbers started to walk away to his relief.

When he got to the school gates, he stood and looked to see if he could see the lady. He saw her jogging down the road towards him. She came up to him and she took her sunglasses off, which were big black things. I recognised her straight away because it was on the front page of the newspaper that she had disappeared. She was Princess Mary in disguise! She was just seeing an old friend without the press on her back.

'At least it wasn't a boring journey to school,' he sighed.

Thomas Doar (12)
Becket RC Comprehensive School

Robin Hood

7pm - King John is settling down for dinner when he gets a phone call.
'Hello, who is this?'
'The man who's following you.'

6pm - 'Tucky, you're outside watching the guards. Zigy, you're distraction and Little John you and I will go for the vault. Hey Zigy, what is the distraction anyway?'
'I'm gonna cut the power that will give you 5 minutes to get in the vault and turn off the lasers.'

6.15pm - 'OK, 3, 2, 1, off.'
Out go the lights.
'Go, go,' says Robin. They crack the code to the vault. John puts out the lasers while Robin opens the safe.
'Robin!'
'What?'
'The cleaners are coming.'
'So?'
'So, they have to be accompanied by security.'
'Quick, hide.'
They hide behind the doors. The cleaners go in the next room and Robin and John grab the diamonds.
'They're beautiful,' says John.
'Yeah, now let's go.'
As they get round the corner they see Robin's ex-wife.
'What's she doing here?'
'She's with King John now.'
'Is that why we were stealing these?'
'Yes, now let's go!'

7pm - 'You'll never catch us, we're already out of the country.'
'How much did you take?'
'40,000,000.'
'Noooooo!'

Luke O'Brien (11)
Becket RC Comprehensive School

The Boot's Nightmare

I was waiting on the platform with my owner. Hugging her leg, I felt her silky soft skin. We sat down on the train. Suddenly the small bumps of the train became aggressive. The passengers screamed, their belongings flew everywhere. I didn't understand what was happening, but I hated it.

Finally the thunderous thuds began to weaken. The loud noises stopped, all I could hear was screaming. My owner just lay lifeless I was tangled up in some cables. Her blood was trickling closer to me.

Two men came into our cabin and took her away. I was left on the train. The next day I was dumped on a rubbish site. It looked and smelt awful, so I decided to get out.

I began to look for an exit. Then I saw a beautiful sight: it was a female boot.

We got talking; she said that she had been here for weeks, trying to get out. We fell in love that very moment. We decided to make ourselves a home. So we began to look for somewhere to live. Then we saw it, an old car with a hole in the side. The perfect door to a perfect home. We found some old curtains and furniture to put in: it was perfect. Now, I am the happiest boot alive. I have a beautiful wife, a lovely house and two wonderful children.

The train crash was the best thing that ever happened to me.

Marie Pearce (12)
Henry Mellish Comprehensive School

The Gresford Disaster

Dear Diary,

I've been trapped down deep in the mine, no one could hear me, the fire was fierce.

Screams, screams, I heard them. The fire roaring, hungry for more. It sounded like a dragon searching for prey. I shouted, 'Lial, Anton and Simon,' over and over again. They had left me. Then silence.

I felt something moving under me. I shouted then I started to get the rubble off my legs and tried to move. I noticed a foot. I helped the man up, it was Anton. I suddenly froze and I thought to myself, *that means they didn't leave me and Simon and Lial are here somewhere*.

Anton was not hurt, he was as fit as a fiddle. I asked if Anton had seen Lial and Simon before the explosion. Anton replied that they had finished earlier so they got to go home.'

Anton and I sat there in silence for about an hour. Then we heard voices, it sounded like the rescue brigade so we started to shout. We heard the rocks and the wood moving. Anton and I helped to move the rocks and the wood out of the way. That's what put a smile on our faces, we were glad we'd been found.

Sharnie Towl (12)
Henry Mellish Comprehensive School

Hip Hopping Hannah And Her Best Mate

A young girl had just awoken as the sun was coming up. This girl was Hannah. She stretched, stood up and looked at herself in the mirror.

'I'm tall, thin and ugly. It's not fair,' she mumbled to herself. To other people she was very pretty, but when she looked at herself she thought she was very ugly.

She turned her music on and started to dress for school, as she was bobbing along with the beat. She loved to dance but only ever in her room. When she was ready she walked to school. She was going to the coffee shop after school with a few friends. She always enjoyed being there.

After school, when she reached the coffee shop, she could see a huge crowd around a girl. She walked over to see her best mate Elizabeth dancing. This was a very weird thing to see.

'Come and join in Hannah,' Elizabeth shouted to her. Hannah just decided to join in. She started to do a really brilliant dance. She had just started this dance when a man walked in. He was in a very grand suit and just stood and watched Hannah.

'Excuse me, do you dance professionally? I would like you to come and work with Missy Elliot and I'm being serious. Meet me tomorrow for the shoot.'

'Oh thank you very much.'

She left school early and earned a lot of money.

'Thanks Elizabeth. It was all down to you.'

'It's all right.'

Lisa-Marie Mckeown (12)
Henry Mellish Comprehensive School

Million Dollar Loss!

On the 10th May an American bank was robbed. One million pounds was stolen by three 16-19 year-olds. The three teenagers walked into the bank, one holding a knife and the other two holding guns. The two gunmen held the guns up to the public and worker and took the money, while the man holding a knife broke the cameras and attacked the security guard.

Thankfully nobody was seriously hurt, but some were injured from dropping on the floor.

All three boys were wearing blue tracksuits. One Umbro and two with a black Puma sign on the back. Nobody yet knows who any of the boys are, but if you know anything about them, please report to your nearest police station or contact us at 01263 9872513 or email us at - Dollarstation@hotmail.com Your help would be appreciated.

Hayleigh Walker-Randle (12)
Henry Mellish Comprehensive School

The Attack Of The Undead Vampire

One stormy night there was a boy called John. He was sitting in his room reading a Darren Shan book. He put his book away. The news came on and the news reporter said, 'Everyone lock your windows and doors, there's something going around biting people's necks and killing them.'

John ran to lock his door. He held his throat and said, 'You're not going to get my neck.' The shutters on his windows started banging. He then got a letter and opened it and screamed, 'Dad!'

His dad said, 'What's wrong?'

His dad read the letter. The letter had 'You're next' in blood written on it.

The other victims received letters like this.

'Dad, call the police, call the army, call anyone, help!'

'Don't worry, someone's probably playing a joke on you.'

That night he thought the thing may be a vampire. So he slept with a stake and a knife under his pillow. Late in the night his window was snapped off the hinges and a deadly voice said, 'I told you you're next.'

John pretended to be asleep. It went to attack him. He pulled the knife out and stabbed the vampire, but it didn't work. John screamed.

Is this the end of John? His courageous dad ran in and shot the vampire with an arrow-gun.

Ashley Huggett (12)
Henry Mellish Comprehensive School

Bubbles In Trouble!

My face pressed to the window, I sniffed back my tears. 'She'll be back,' I told myself. I was worried about my fluffy white cat Bubbles. Bubbles had been missing for three hours. She'd never gone astray before. Our neighbours were having new decking laid. Bubbles had been spooked out by all the noise and disappeared. Ever since I had picked out Bubbles at the cat home we'd been inseparable. I knew I'd be heartbroken if anything had happened to her.

As days passed, me and my mum plastered posters across the area, knocked on doors, even my mum offered a £100 reward. But there was no sign of my beloved Bubbles. Sometimes I'd hear her in the garden. I prayed she'd be all right.

Eight long weeks passed, then one day our neighbour called round. 'I think I've found Bubbles,' he grinned. He'd heard miaowing coming from his new decking. I rushed into his garden. My heart was thumping. As I peered through the gaps in the oak decking, I heard a familiar sound.

'Bubbles!' I yelled. She'd got trapped during the construction work. I had heard her after all. As the neighbour removed a board Bubbles shot into my arms. She was trembling, filthy, but alive. At home she gulped down food and water. I wrapped her in a blanket. Four shampoos later, her fur was white again. A vet checked her over too.

'It's a miracle,' he told us. Bubbles had survived on just rain water and insects. What a tough pussycat!

Casey Wombwell (12)
Henry Mellish Comprehensive School

Drama Teenz

Shocking!

A terrible incident left two dead and many injured. Yesterday afternoon at about 2.15 a madman entered All Nations hairdressers and took two lives. Six-year-old Tina and twenty-year-old Tyler were killed at the scene. They were killed by a rifle at the cramped shop. Tina was shot at point blank in the head and died straight away while Tyler was shot six times from a short distance, twice in the stomach, once in her lung and three shots to the head. She died after the last three shots. So many were injured as the masked man shot randomly around the room before shooting himself. Nobody knows the reason for this man's rage or why he chose that shop.

A passer-by (who doesn't want to be named) said he heard the shots and was frozen to the spot. He didn't know exactly where they were coming from but he knew they were close. Another onlooker (Andre from Hyson Green) said, 'At first I thought they were fireworks but I couldn't see anything in the sky and they were going too quick'.

The families of Tyler and Tina are devastated. Tyler's mother, Dawn, 42 says, 'We just want to know why this man took away our precious daughter's life so we can try and get on with our lives. I keep thinking that she's going to walk through the door at any moment, but then I remember the awful truth'.

The killer, named Jack, 33 also died at the scene. His family declined to comment.

Nyala Skerritt (13)
Henry Mellish Comprehensive School

Winning The Lottery

The Adams family had just brought a lottery ticket as it was a triple rollover that night. They always brought a ticket, but they never won anything. Saturday night had arrived. The whole family sat around the telly at quarter past seven, just before the lottery started to begin. The programme came on, a band played their music, then the draw began. First number was twelve, then twenty, then thirty-five, then seven, then nineteen, then forty-one and the bonus ball was five. The Adams family had matched all six numbers. The family were all cheering and joyful. Mr Adams rang a number on the back of the ticket.

The following day a lady came around the house to confirm the ticket was correct, which it was. The lady handed over a cheque for £7.8 million.

The next day the family gave the house away. They moved into a mansion and sent their son to boarding school.

After a month, the family got bored of the money, so they decided to buy their old house back, which they did. They got all the money which they had changed into notes, kept £20,000 for themselves, gave over £3 million to charities, then threw the money off the highest place in the country. They then got back into their normal lives as it was before. They never did the lottery again.

Moral: money doesn't always make you happy.

Joe Robinson (13)
Henry Mellish Comprehensive School

Jacob And The Dragon

The great King Michael was a horrid, twisted man who had a son called Jacob. Jacob's mother had broken up with his father and they lived in separate homes. When Jacob became nineteen, his father set him a task.

'If you kill the legendary dragon that is killing my men, I will crown you the king. If you fail, I'll burn down your house while your mother is asleep. You must go to Fire Cavern which is just north from here. If you kill the dragon, bring back the head in this bag.'

So along went the bravest man to Fire Cavern. As he climbed up the raging rock, an inferno of flames erupted out of the cavern. As the dragon peered out, its claws as sharp as a razor ripped away at the dead bodies. Its gleaming gold eyes glistened and moved like tiny diamonds glistening in the night sky.

He dodged the erupting flames as they engulfed his shield. He climbed on the vicious beast and stabbed it in the neck, but the scales were too hard and the sword simply snapped into two. He jabbed again with his jagged blade and the dragon's blood rushed like a fountain spraying upwards.

The next day he returned home and his house was burnt down. He went straight to the palace

His father came rushing out, screaming, 'You should be dead.'

Jacob became king and ordered his father to be killed because of the murder he'd committed.

Luke Brown (13)
Henry Mellish Comprehensive School

My Advice For A Lonely Heart

Monday

You will have a man's heart within a few months. Many people will question your choice, but follow your heart. Do not let anybody stand in your way! You should be yourself.

Tuesday

Look to the future, not behind you. Find a hobby to which you prefer and you will enjoy. You will find true love. If you see somebody who you like, do not approach them, let them come to you.

Wednesday

Mind what you say to people as it may backfire on your love life. Many people will have been affected with your advice. Look beyond what you see and it will be very bright.

Thursday

Enjoy your life. Look to what you think is right. Do not believe in love at first sight, as it could backfire and seriously harm your feelings and the way of your lifestyle.

Friday

Lose yourself in a really good book. Enjoy the free time to yourself, as you will have no free time. You will be going on a long trip somewhere exotic.

Saturday

Go out with a mate to the cinema and you will find your man. He will be slow but very alert with his surroundings.

Do not back away as he will get the wrong impression.

Sunday

When you go out, look over your right shoulder. There will be a man staring at you. Wave just a little.

Kimberley Gough (13)
Henry Mellish Comprehensive School

The Night Of The Hurricane

Day after day, month after month, the sun shone from a sky of deep blue. But all of this was going to change. I was inside all day waiting for the hurricane to arrive. Then with a bang, the lightning flashed. The hurricane had arrived with dark clouds forming, covering the pale blue sky. The rain was calling murder, soaking the ground and drenching the plants, overflowing the roads, rivers and the ponds. How fast the water gathered, filling the canals and the fields; the vast cultivation where the crops were lush and green, now covered by water. More lightning!

I was beginning to get petrified; frightened, fearful, worried and nervous all at the same time. I tried to wrap myself more warmly into the blanket but it wasn't big enough. I shielded myself from the leaves flying in from beneath the door, watching the water rising each second, getting closer and closer to my bed. Hoping that this was a dream, praying that this would end; wishing that I was somewhere else.

Except this wasn't a dream, it wouldn't end and it was happening to me. I could hear a gust of wind singing into my ears which sent me to sleep.

I woke up in the still cold hours of the morning, stiff, uncomfortable and trembling. I went outside and I found that my garden had suffered severely from the hurricane. Several of the finest blooms were laid pathetically destroyed on the muddy path. What a scene to behold.

Krissie Suban (12)
Henry Mellish Comprehensive School

The Lion's Head

It was a breezy night. I could hear a sound coming from the hallway. I got up, yet I didn't want to. It was like my feet were walking on their own. I walked downstairs and grabbed a torch. I didn't know where I was going but my feet did. I opened the front door and walked outside. My house was breezier than outside. The stones on the floor made my feet hurt, yet I still was walking. I walked to the beachside, the water was hitting my face.

I stopped when I came to a big old house. The gate had a lion's head on it. It started to thunder and rain. I opened the gate and walked up to the front door and knocked on it. Nobody answered it. I went to knock again when the door opened on its own. I started to sweat in this house. I started to walk faster. It was like someone had tied a piece of rope around me and was pulling me up the stairs.

I got to the top of the stairs. I felt faint. I saw something from the corner of my eye. I turned round to see someone staring at me. I screamed and grabbed his top, then everything went black.

I opened my eyes. Mum said I was dreaming, but when she went out of the room, I saw in my hands I had a torch.

'It really happened,' I said to myself.

Danielle Strickson (12)
Henry Mellish Comprehensive School

The Sun

Manchester United 4 - 2 Arsenal

Everybody knew it would be a make or break game. These teams hated each other so it would be a dramatic game and it was. Firstly, Arsenal walked on the pitch very smug and confident and Manchester United walked onto the pitch, nervous and challenged. As they started the game, Arsenal looked the better team with some through balls and after 27 minutes it paid off; bad marking from United left Viera with a free header, 1-0. Then a great run from Ronaldo to the equaliser, good ball to Ryan Giggs and he finished it. Then a couple of bad tackles got some bookings. Rooney and Pires went into the ref's book. Then a good run by Lauren left Heinze on his bum and then a ball to Bergkamp made it 2-1 Arsenal, half-time.

Then Man U came out fighting, a great cross by Giggs found Ronaldo - 2-2, the game was on. The fans were singing and the atmosphere was ecstatic. Then Ronaldo took two players on and hit a screamer 3-2. From 2-1 down United turned it on a head. Then two fine saves by the United keeper kept them in it and as they all threw the Arsenal men up, United caught them on the break and John O'Shea finished them with a 94-minute chip. Arsenal have not lost a game now so they have their title chance.

Michael Tyers (13)
Henry Mellish Comprehensive School

Appendix Horror

I was getting ready for a party. When we got there we all sat down, then me, my brother and three sisters, and our friends started a game of 'dobby' so I ran and did not stop. Then I started to get a pain in my right side so I sat down. I was in agony and my mum thought it was cramp. My mum took me outside for some fresh air, but it did not help.

My dad said, 'Shall we take him to his grandma's?' and they did.

My dad phoned NHS and they didn't know what it was so they said they would phone us back. I was sick and it was a greeny colour, so we went to the NHS. When I got there I had to have a bladder test.

After that we went to the hospital. They put me in a bed. After that they took a blood test, then they put me on a drip and I could not eat for three days. They said it was appendicitis so they needed to change the drip every day.

The day after that they did the operation to take my appendix out. They took me in and when I woke up, my mum was there waiting for me. The next day I was allowed to go home but I had to wait for my medicine before I went home.

Lee Read (11)
Henry Mellish Comprehensive School

What Shall I Do?

There was a girl who woke up one day with a problem. 'Who shall I go with, Chantelle or Lisa? I don't know! I like them both,' Nedean shouted at the top of her voice. 'I wish I could do both,' she said as she threw herself onto the settee.

This poor little girl has been asked to go to a sleepover with Chantelle or to go to a party with Lisa. She then decided to ring them both up and have a three-way conversation.

'Deal!'

They made a decision for them all to go to the party with Lisa and then to go the sleepover with Chantelle.

'It will be great,' she said to herself.

She went to her friend Lisa's house, ready for the party but she took clean clothes to wear the next day when she went home.

They all sat and had a little chat before starting, because everything was ready and there was still an hour left till the party started.

They chatted for about half an hour as they drank a cup of tea.

At 6pm they started the party. At first people just waited for their other friends to get there so that they could have a good time together.

Danielle, Jordan and Nelly were at the party. They also went to the sleepover.

The party finished at 8pm. They all went back to Chantelle's house, got a scary movie and then watched it.

Nedean Betteridge (12)
Henry Mellish Comprehensive School

Sleeping Beauty Retold

Once upon a time there lived a king and queen who lived in a pink and sparkling castle. It was Princess Mea's christening and everyone had an invitation except the evil witch. Everyone brought gifts, even the three fairies. The fairies gave gifts of beauty, love and strength. The three fairies took Princess Mea into the forest so the wicked witch wouldn't find her.

The years flew by and it was Princess Mea's sixteenth birthday and the three fairies were organising a surprise birthday party for her. While they were planning the party, they sent her in the forest to pick some flowers. Then, to her surprise, she heard a man singing. It sounded like a voice she had heard before. It was a prince offering to dance with her, but she didn't talk to strangers so she ran back to the cottage. When she got back, the fairies weren't there.

Suddenly, a black mist covered the cottage. The lovely sound of the birds singing was taken over by the sound of a loud cackle. It was the evil witch coming to take her away. The cottage was now empty. The princess was then put in a trance and the witch led her down a long flight of stairs. She took her to a big, empty room with a spindle wheel which the princess pricked her finger on and began to bleed. She then collapsed into a deep sleep for 100 years ...

Tiffany Colagiovanni (12)
Henry Mellish Comprehensive School

Dominican Convent

It was my first day at Dominican Convent. I was really nervous because I did not know anyone. I was shown to my classroom that I was in. There was a huge woman who looked mean. Everyone was quiet and staring at me. I felt really sick. The teacher came to me and introduced herself. She showed me where to sit. I sat next to this kind girl.

We started with the maths lesson. She helped me but I still did not understand the work. We then had swimming for PE. I was surprised that they had three swimming pools. Luckily they had a spare costume for me. We got changed, then we swam for an hour. The water was freezing cold. When we finished, we had lunch for an hour. I had a burger and chips. When we had finished our lunch we went to English. It was really boring because the teacher kept talking.

We finally had a library lesson. It was quite boring but it was better than English. After the library lesson we went home. It was a great first day after all. My best lesson was swimming. I also had a new best friend called Patience.

Shirley Kutadzaushe (11)
Henry Mellish Comprehensive School

Jack And The Beanstalk

Once upon a time, there was a little boy who lived with his mother in a faraway cottage. They struggled as there was no one to work for. All they had was a cow.

'Now Jack, go and sell that cow for three shillings,' said Jack's mother.

Jack set off to find someone to buy his cow. He passed a rich person. 'Would you like to buy my cow?' Jack asked.

'Nope,' said the rich person.

'Please, Sir, please,' Jack begged.

'Did you just hear me? No,' the man yelled.

Jack just walked away.

The sun had started going down. Then a strange-looking man came.

'Erm, would you like to buy my cow for ...' Jack said.

'I'll buy it off you for three magic beans,' the man interrupted.

'Well, OK,' Jack agreed. He turned around to thank the man, but he was gone. Jack decided to stop wondering where the man had gone and started heading home. Jack finally got home. 'Mum, Mum, I sold that cow,' Jack shouted.

Jack's mum jumped with joy. 'How much? How much?' she asked.

'Three magic beans,' he smiled.

'What? Beans?' Her face filled with rage. She took the beans and chucked them.

The sun came back up. Jack looked out of his window and there was a huge beanstalk so he ran down into the garden. He stood there in shock. 'Mum, look at this,' Jack yelled.

'What now?' Jack's mum said. 'Well, what are you waiting for? Get climbing. Look at them beans at the top.' Jack's mother licked her lips.

'OK,' Jack sighed. He started climbing. Just as he reached the top he heard a strange noise. He got to the top and there was a huge castle.

Jack got to the door and used all his strength to open the door. There was a giant. Jack walked further, then he heard the giant speak.

'Fe, fi, fo, fum, I smell the blood of an Englishman,' the giant said, gazing at Jack.

Jack ran down the beanstalk. 'Mum, chop the stalk down,' Jack panicked.

His mum got the axe and chopped the beanstalk down and the giant fell to his death.

Ashley Leighton (12)
Henry Mellish Comprehensive School

My Best Holiday

I felt the engine running under my feet. My ears started popping, my brother's ears too. I felt glad when we were up. Off to Mexico we went, ten and a half hours' flight it had taken. I fell asleep as there was nothing to do, so I dreamed a wonderful dream. I woke up; there I was getting ready to get off the plane.

There I stood near the five star hotels; beautiful view, hot weather, white sand and the deep blue sea.

My dad went off for a walk. When he came back he said, 'There's a children's club down there.'

My brother and I followed him. There were two teachers there and no children, so we went to the restaurant. After that we went swimming, played on the beach and went canoeing. The canoeing was great - I nearly fell out.

On the tenth day it was my brother's birthday. My mum had brought his cards on holiday for him. He opened some presents on holiday. We were on holiday for fourteen days. We did not want to go back.

'I love it here, I don't want to go,' I said.

We went on the plane again. The engine was under my feet and my ears were popping. That was my holiday to Mexico.

Jessie Harrison (12)
Henry Mellish Comprehensive School

A Miracle

'Do you think this is safe, Rachael?' asked Megan.

'Why, are you scared?' said Rachael, laughing.

It was dark. Midnight. The two best friends were walking along a path. Suddenly Megan had a full flashback of a big house.

'Are you alright, Megan?' Rachael asked.

Megan would not move, not one finger would move either. Megan was as solid as a statue.

'Has Megan fainted or even died just standing up?' Rachael asked herself. She started to walk along the path and then ... she got the same flashback herself, but she didn't faint or die standing up.

She carried on walking along the creepy old path, crying because she'd lost her bestest friend ever.

Sooner or later, she got the same flashback again, then, when the flashback finished, she was standing in front of the house!

When she went into the house, she was standing in the hallway. It looked dull and cobwebs were in each corner of the ceiling. 'This house must be old,' Rachael said to herself.

Then there was a great big bang on the door she was standing in front of, but she didn't know what it was. Before she could open the door, the monster behind it grabbed her in. She couldn't breathe. It was a ghost, but before she turned into a ghost something saved her. She didn't know what had saved her, but we will find out next time.

Nikki Edwards (12)
Henry Mellish Comprehensive School

Falling In Love!

'Goodbye,' the boy said to the heartbroken girl.

As tears rolled down her face, she remembered how he'd stolen her heart.

He walked past her window and her eyes fell from the TV and lay on him. Her heart was on her knee.

Then the next thing that hit her was the kiss. It was like Heaven had opened and pulled her up. Then the great kiss ended and she was back watching a video in the dark.

Yet she was hearing the words 'goodbye'. As the van pulled away, her heart was taken too.

She ran inside, longing to be in his arms.

She sat feeling lost, then a great smile came on her face as she remembered his jacket upstairs.

She put it on and felt his arms holding her close.

Kayleigh Alicia Potter (16)
Henry Mellish Comprehensive School

Never Together Again

My sister and I are Siamese twins. We were born like it and had been like it for 24 years. But 2 years, 3 months, 1 week and 4 days ago we had one of the strangest days of our lives - but who's counting?

It was a Saturday and for 3 months I had been dreading this day, but Lizzie wasn't, she was so excited she couldn't sleep the night before and I should know. We got up about 8.30, had a shower, got dressed and packed our bags ready to leave at 12.00. The taxi arrived just in time and took us to our destination.

When we got there we signed in (ignoring the sarcastic comments made by the other people in the waiting room), then took a seat. Our names were called and we were taken down a long corridor to a room with a double bed and a curtain going all the way around the bed. The woman that led us there then gave us 2 gowns and asked us to change into them, so we did.

10 to 15 minutes later, a man walked in and introduced himself. He was very kind. We were then told to lie on the bed as another man came in with a woman. I gripped Lizzie's hand quite tight and she gave me a reassuring smile which helped but still didn't take the butterflies out of my stomach. The 2 men and the woman then wheeled the bed down through many corridors and finally into a large room. It had a massive light in the centre which hung quite low down and a lot of small silver tables surrounding us with things on I didn't like the look of. The man then injected both me and Lizzie with a needle and asked us to count backwards from ten. Lizzie got to 6 and I got to 4.

Many hours later I woke up and felt as light as a feather and as sick and dizzy as though I was hungover. Lizzie was still asleep. I called her name but she still didn't wake. The man came in and explained.

'Well, Chantelle, the operation was a success and you should make a full recovery in about a week or so.'

Then I remembered what had just happened. At first I thought, *no, it can't be*, but when I looked at Lizzie she seemed a million miles away, yet she was only 3 metres away.

'We did it, Chantelle, we've been separated!'

I wanted to cry but I knew I had to be strong for Lizzie.

The next few days were tough but together we got through it. I was sad in a way, I no longer have Lizzie to depend on to keep me standing straight. But I was also happy as we were no longer the circus freaks everyone made us out to be!

Rebecca Bancroft (12)
Redhill Comprehensive School

A Day In The Life Of An Evacuee

The train began to chug along the rickety track as the city and the bombed wrecks faded away. Soon we were on our way through greenery and foliage as the sun slipped away and welcomed the night.

I pulled down the blackout curtains, sealing me in the compartment. I sat on the cushioned seats, immersed in my thoughts until I fell into a deep, though unsettled slumber.

I awoke, though the darkness of early morning lingered over the train. My bunches hung limply over my shoulders and dark bags, like storm clouds, surrounded my eyes, the sign of the past few sleepless nights.

Everything had happened so quickly over the past week. First Mother told me I was being evacuated, away from the bombs in London, then I foolishly ran away as the thought of going away to Scotland scared me. Whilst Mother was looking for me, there was an air raid. I feel so selfish. I can't change what happened now, it is all my fault - my mother is now dead.

I tried to imagine what it would be like in Scotland, however all I can picture is lots of people in kilts with bagpipes, fiery orange hair and a strong accent. That was the most stereotypical image I could have thought of but I had no idea what to expect.

As the train approached the station, I noticed the thick mesh of grey clouds release a heavy blanket of rain, soaking all of the people on the platform. The brakes squeaked as the train came to a halt, ending the long and tiresome journey.

On the platform I saw an array of faces. Some were trying to look smiley and welcoming, but failed in doing so. Others looked blank with slate-grey expressions, as if they didn't know what to say, like they felt sorry for us. Sympathy was the last thing I needed.

I stepped out of the train and gazed up at the grim complexion of the sky. The downpour had stopped, although it still kept the sun hidden as though it was a prisoner of the storm. My gas mask box made my neck ache and my suitcase felt like lead. I took a deep breath and held my head up high. I tried to muster a smile. I had to make a good impression.

A tall, dark-haired woman in a smart suit began to pair up children with families, calling in her fiery tone numbers and names. '087612, Lucy Edwards.'

I walked over to her cautiously, afraid of her. As I got closer, I noticed her hair was combed so tightly to her head her eyes almost popped under the strain.

'Over there,' she pointed.

'Right then, this is your room, any questions? No? Good. Dinner will be on the table at six o'clock and bedtime is at eight.'

'Thank you,' I replied shyly. When she left, I sat on my bed. I felt my eyes prick, then the tears came. They slid down my cheeks like a cascading waterfall. I wiped my streaming eyes and mopped my nose.

When I finally arrived downstairs, Mrs Carter, my 'new' mother, barked at me to set the table. As I laid the lacy cloth, my eyes scanned the walls and a portrait of a newly married couple caught my attention. The young woman's perplexing brown eyes met with mine and I stood for a moment examining the picture. I was brought back to reality by Mrs Carter calling me to the kitchen.

Whilst we were having dinner, the atmosphere was tense. There was definitely an air of dislike coming from Mrs Carter, as though I was an unwelcome intruder. I went through to the kitchen and washed my plate.

'Get to bed now please. I expect you to be up early doing your chores. Goodnight.'

Whilst I was washing my face, the cool splash of water made me remember home. The thought stayed with me as I lay down on the frilly blankets and I rested my head on the pillow. I wanted to go back and I tried to imagine after the war when Father would be home and we would try to pick up the pieces of the passing away of my mother. As my eyelids began to shut I heard the twelve chimes of the ornamental clock on the mantelpiece. My last thoughts were, *tomorrow's another day*.

Laura Bray (12)
Redhill Comprehensive School

A Day In The Life Of An Evacuee - War Runaway

As we huddle together, my little brother weeps, cold and hungry. We didn't want to be evacuated up here to Wales, so we ran away. The only provisions we took were a few apples, a couple of slices of bread and all we had to keep us warm was a ragged, patched blanket. Now I know that I'd much rather be sat in front of the fire in Wales than out here in the cold, but we can't go back. We're lost.

In the morning I awake to the whistling of the birds and the soft breeze brushing past my face. I stand up to stretch my arms and legs. Edward (my brother) is still asleep. I hear a faint trickling sound which must be a stream. I wake Edward up, we eat a small red apple between us. Then we go in search of the stream, dodging in and out of the trees, searching through the woods as the sound gets louder. After walking for around 10 minutes we find the stream. Edward and myself wash our grubby faces and sweaty armpits, then carry on to find a way out of the woods.

We found a small, narrow footpath that we're still following now. We've walked a long way and Edward is getting hungry and weak as we've only had half an apple to eat all day. I tell him he can't have any food because we haven't got enough to last us, so we carry on going.

'Can we have a rest now?' asks Edward, moaning.

'Look,' I say, 'I'm sure we'll be out of here soon. We can have a rest then.'

We carry on going quietly, when suddenly I hear a loud thud. I turn around but can't see Edward. The sky is navy blue now and it makes it even harder to see. I look down and see his figure lying there, still. So still that I think he's dead. I try to wake him up, but he won't. I feel his pulse. Thank God, he's still alive.

When it gets lighter I go to find help. I find my way out of the woods, unravelling my knitted cardigan so I can find my way back. I carry on the footpath which leads into a huge field which is by a narrow road. As I run forwards I see Mr and Mrs Jones (our evacuee guardians) looking very upset and next to them is a police officer and his car. I rush towards them, waving my arms frantically, calling, *'Help! Help! Help!'*

Mrs Jones turns around, spots me and runs towards me with her arms wide open. 'What is the matter?' she asks me as I'm sobbing.

'It's Edward, he's unconscious in the woods over there!'

Mr Jones and the police officer come running over as Mrs Jones beckons them. Mrs Jones tells them about Edward and we go rushing back through the woods, following the pink wool trail until we reach Edward. Mr Jones and the police officer carry him back to the car.

Edward is still in hospital but should be out soon as he is recovering fast. We've got to stay in Wales until the war is over, but I don't mind because Mr and Mrs Jones are really kind, although I miss Mother. I sent her a letter two days ago, but she hasn't replied. I hope she is alright.

Sophie Macmillan (12)
Redhill Comprehensive School

A Day In The Life Of A Posh Poodle

My eyes slowly opened, I saw pink everywhere, pink walls, pink toys, pink carpet. Once my eyes had adjusted to the light I slowly stood up on my pink fluffy pillow.

I then wandered out the door and into the room opposite. I started barking and jumped onto the bed.

'Calm down, Pixie! Calm down,' said the woman lying in the bed. The woman sat up in bed and rang a little silver bell with dogs on it.

Just then a young man entered. 'Yes, M'lady?' said the butler.

'Please go and feed Pixie and also dress her,' replied the woman.

'As you wish. Come on, Pixie,' said the butler.

I quickly followed him downstairs. We entered a big room with a big bath, lots of bottles and beauty products, food and accessories. In the corner of the room was a dog bowl and inside the dog bowl was my favourite dog food, IAMS meaty chunks. I ate it up in an instant. I was then put into the dog bath. The butler then scrubbed me to death with this really prickly brush that hurt a bit. I then got out of the bath and shook myself dry, but just to make sure I was dry, the butler dried me with the blow dryer. He then got out a lovely pink fur jewellery box. He opened it and inside was a beautiful silver collar with a heart-shaped pendant on with my name, 'Pixie', on it. The butler gently placed it around my neck and buckled it together. It felt so soft against my fur. I quickly looked in the mirror, I looked beautiful.

Just then my owner walked in the room and clipped my dog lead onto my collar. 'Come on, Pixie, we're going for a walk around the lake,' said my owner.

We left without another word. She quickly opened the main door and we exited the house. There was a path around the lake that we followed every day. The walk lasted about an hour. The lake was beautiful with lots of greenery and nature.

Once we had got back to the house it was time for dinner. I had IAMS meaty chunks again, I also had some milk. I rather like milk, even though I'm a dog.

When I had finished licking my lips, my owner took me to a pet shop. I was going to get a new bed as the one I have at the moment is a bit out of fashion. We had a look around, there were lots of different things there. There were lots of colours. I sat on lots of different cushions. The one I eventually decided to get was a bright pink and purple striped, with like a barrier around so I was snugly and warm. I also got some more bows for my fur. (My owner's very kind.)

When we returned home it was very late, so I quickly stripped down of all my accessories. I was given a drop of milk before I went to bed. The butler laid out my new bed in my room. I quickly bounced on it and fell asleep, wondering what I was going to do tomorrow.

Laura Harvey (11)
Redhill Comprehensive School

The Dragon And George

The dragon swooped lower with the effortlessness of the experienced, her tail danced on the breeze like a kite. Her unwary chick rode inexpertly on the northern wind. Below a march of Homo sapiens, not common occurrences in this desolate part of England. Her chick dived down, too far down, it was an army with knights, footmen and ... archers. The arrows ripped his juvenile wings, like rock through wet paper; his body plummeted towards the ground out of its owner's control. The bloodthirsty knights pounced on her defenceless baby. She dived, her slipstream tearing at her wings. No. He was dead. The mother dragon moaned a heart-melting moan, she craved blood, the blood of her chick's murderers.

In a nearby pub, The Nags Head, a couple of farmers were having a family get-together (you know the sort, with conversation topics like; what good is the thieving business for old Henry?), one of the people there was fat old Uncle George, but if you called him this you would get a ding round the earhole. George was happily enjoying getting seriously drunk when a town crier entered.

'Hesh a posh oldsh twerpsh!' George muttered.

'Hear ye! Hear ye!' the town crier cried. 'The princess has been tied to a rock outside the dragon's cave, we need one of you to go and save her!'

George stood up with a grating of a chair. 'Whysh did ya gosh an' tie up Her Majestysh if you just wan' ussh to go an' rescue hersh?'

'Oh no,' whispered our William.

'It looks like we have a volunteer!' rumbled the town crier.

'Thatsh righ', fancy pansh, stick thatsh up your bobbin' hat an' smokesh itsh! Thish time tomz I will be knowsh as Georgesh the Drogonsh Slayer!'

A soft groaning came from the mouth of the dragon's lair. The princess moved slightly, jostling the chains that bound her to the fang-shaped rock outside the dragon's cave.

A soft noise on the breeze of someone singing and the faint linger of alcohol. 'Shining a hash dingle derbysh and a hay dingle daysh ... hee ... hee!'

The groaning stopped suddenly with surprising abruptness, a sharp intake of breath, a sniff ... then ... an ear-ripping roar echoed off the surrounding natural stone walls, but hidden deep within the roar was intense pain.

The dragon charged out of the cave, her joints moved without the ease they had once. George had been camping out, with only 3 barrels of beer for company. The dragon was the size of two horses and had a wingspan of 3m. Arrow holes littered her wings, denying her flight. Scars criss-crossed her body from a fight in which she had lost her chick. She charged through the barrels without grace.

George had answered the call of nature behind a bush. The beer gushed over the broken body, she opened her mouth in surprise, the foul liquid rushed down her throat. The alcohol overloaded her tottering heart and pushed it over the edge. The dragon was drawn out by despair and lack of food, but the alcohol poisoned her fragile heart and killed her. She moaned as the tool of death seeped away, a whisper escaped her lips as she collapsed. Any dragon nearby would have heard a sound on the wind.

'I am coming, my chick.'

Siân Brooke (11)
Redhill Comprehensive School

Dragon Wars: The Beginning

Many years ago, before time, there lived three generations of elves, dwarves and men. For many years they had lived together in peace until the invasion started. All turned black over Draconia as the rain began to fall. Sounds of howling and pounding could be heard in the air. As it started to become louder, flames were seen in the atmosphere that were generated by giant shadow-like figures which could fly. Then they landed in the darkest part of Draconia, the Dark Regions. Draconia now faced a problem for the first time. They now had an enemy.

North of the Dark Regions lay Calinor, land of men. The lord of men was wise, but even he could not work out what had happened. Caliendran the lord asked for his son, Maliencran.

'Father, what has happened? Who is it?' asked Maliencran.

'Do not worry my son,' answered the lord. 'We must first find out if they are here to become friends or enemies. We will send a messenger to find out.'

'Would you like me to send one now, Father?' asked Maliencran.

His father soon replied, 'No, not now. We shall wait until sunrise. It will be safer then.'

At sunrise, the lord sent a messenger to the gate of the Dark Regions.

The messenger rode through the Black Gem mountains towards the gate and shouted aloud, 'In the name of Lord Caliendran, are you friend or foe?'

There was silence for awhile until a whistle came through the air. The messenger was killed.

After a week, the lord sent a knight to check on the arrival of the messenger, only to find a rotting body on the floor. The knight swiftly rode back to Calinor with the news for the lord. When he arrived he informed Caliendran. The lord now knew why they had come. To conquer. He sent a message to the elf lord, Kiren, and to Gandfoug, lord of the dwarves. They both then sent their sons to Calinor to discuss the dilemma. At the meeting was Maliencran of men, Orlandas of elves and Randfoug of dwarves. They discussed battle plans, where the battle was to take place and who would lead, but they were stuck on one problem - who the enemy were.

Randfoug decided he should go to the gate to look for clues to see who the enemy were because he was an expert in all living things and history.

Randfoug travelled to the gate with Maliencran to search for answers. He soon found an engraving in the wall. It was of the dragon language.

'They are dragons!' exclaimed Randfoug. 'They are dragons.'

'How do you know?' asked Maliencran. 'They could have been engraved years ago.'

'The rock is still clean and the tool was left here. Look,' answered Randfoug.

'OK then, what does it say?' asked Maliencran.

'It says that this is the land of dragons and Lord Dalfang. Anyone who disturbs us or enters will suffer the consequences,' replied Randfoug.

'We must inform my father!' exclaimed Maliencran.

Two days later they both arrived at Calinor. All the lords had gathered in the meeting room for the news. Randfoug explained who the enemy were and the lords were astonished, as dragons had only been at Draconia once and that was thousands of years ago.

'We shall prepare for battle in three days. Round up all soldiers and take them to the gate. Keep your distance though, they could strike,' shouted Caliendran.

Three days had passed with the army all set and ready. The men were at the front with their heavy swords and shields, next the dwarves with their giant axes and lastly the elves with their long sight and bows and arrows. The gates then gave a creak and opened with one dragon walking out in the direction of Lord Caliendran. It was Lord Dalfang.

Lord Dalfang asked him, 'Why do you trouble us? We come here to settle not to fight.'

'Then why did you kill my messenger?' asked Caliendran violently.

'He insulted us by asking if we were friend or foe. Now please let us be to our own doing,' replied Dalfang.

'Then why the message on the wall?' asked Caliendran.

'We just do not want anyone to disturb us. Now please leave,' said Dalfang.

'All right. We will leave you to your own doing,' said Caliendran. The lord ordered the troops to return to their homeland.

Dalfang returned into the Dark Regions with a grin on his face. 'We will attack at nightfall and take over Draconia like we did to the other three countries. All shall perish!' cackled Dalfang as the gates shut. 'Draconia will be mine!'

Matt McAdam (12)
Redhill Comprehensive School

Kidnap! What Really Happened?

Reporter Kate Johnson interviewed kidnapper Charles Parker and his victim, Victoria Robson. On the 5th August 2027, Charles kidnapped Victoria from her hometown of Rollerville. For years we have not been able to discover why Charles never harmed or held Victoria against her own will. Hopefully today, the 7th September 2030, we will find out.

Kate: 'Why did you kidnap Victoria all those years ago?'
Charles: 'Well, I didn't want to hurt her. I just wanted to teach her a lesson. I wanted to teach her a lesson because about a month before, Victoria and her friends came into my shop and broke many of my computers and I didn't know why.'
Victoria: 'I never touched your stupid computers.'
Charles: 'You did, I saw you.'
Kate: 'Enough, enough! Victoria, what happened when Charles kidnapped you?'
Victoria: 'I was walking down to my friend's house as you do, when this man grabbed me from behind. I screamed but he put his hand over my mouth. I was so scared.'
Kate: 'Is this true?'
Charles: 'Yes, I didn't mean too, I just didn't want to attract anyone's attention.'
Kate: 'If you didn't want to hurt her, why did you kidnap her?'
Charles: 'Well, like I said before, I wanted to teach her a lesson.'
Kate: 'Why didn't you go to the police?'
Victoria: 'He didn't go to the police because he knew I was innocent!'
Charles: 'Shut up. I did go to the police but they didn't believe me!'
Kate: 'So you decided to take the law into your own hands?'
Charles: 'Yes. I know I shouldn't have but I couldn't help it. I hated her so much.'
Kate: 'Why didn't you hurt her if you hated her so much?'
Charles: 'I was going to but I couldn't bring myself to do so.'
Kate: 'Thank you Charles. Victoria, your turn. Where did he take you once he had kidnapped you?'
Victoria: 'I don't know, it was a long way away though. He put me in the back of a van, it had no windows, it was cold and damp. No light found its way in. I was terrified!'
Kate: 'Charles, are you OK?'
Charles: 'It's all true. I just can't believe it though.'
Kate: 'OK Charles, don't worry. Victoria, did Charles hurt you?'
Victoria: 'No.'

Kate: 'Could you have left at any time?'
Victoria: 'Yes.'
Kate: 'Why didn't you?'
Victoria: 'I don't know, I think I felt sorry for him.'
Charles: 'So you should have. You ruined my business.'
Kate: 'I think we will stop there before there is a fight.'

Hannah Spencer (11)
Redhill Comprehensive School

World War III - The Rise Of Hitler

It's 2098 and robots are at war with humans, mutants and aliens! It started in 2097 because of a robot called Hitler. He was the greatest of robots. He was so powerful that we thought that we couldn't win the war, until he came along. He was powerful, giant and the scariest mutant you would have ever seen in your life. His name was Under Demon. He ruled the underworld. The president of Earth asked him to lead his army to victory. So the mutant got armoured up and set off to the battlefield.

They finally got to the battlefield on their super rockets. They saw the robots over the horizon and the leader of the Earth launched a boulder at the opponents and killed them straight away. The army were attacking the enemy before they got over the hill. The robots returned the attack with the hi-tech laser bomb. The mutant charged at the millions of machines.

The robots backed off and Hitler stood forward with no fear. The mutant shot Hitler with a cybotronic ray gun, but he soon got up and returned the shot with a turbo-charged laser. They started shooting but nothing would stop any of them. The armies crept forwards and attacked each other trying not to get crushed.

After a couple of hours both of the armies were dead except for the mutant and Hitler. Under Demon thought that nothing would stop him. So he turned Hitler around and pulled open his main drive and started ripping out his main wires. Soon after he was switched off. And just for proof Under Demon took Hitler's head and showed it to the galaxy.

After the war the universe declared peace.

Bradley Nightingale (11)
Redhill Comprehensive School

Killer Flower … !

The Irish Ditty Flower is extremely dangerous. *It kills.*

The flower started killing in the early hours of Saturday 18th February 2004. It started in Tony Blair's office by killing him and his wife. So far it has killed over 1,000,000 people. It just won't stop.

The flower works by biting its victim 6 times, then leaves its deadly poison to work. The symptoms are: bright green spots, feeling sick, dizziness and green bloodshot eyes. You will feel the pain for 6 days before you die (a day for every bite).

There are only 24 Irish Ditty flowers left in the whole world!

The only way to kill the flower is to make it eat a poisonous snake! No one would dare to touch a poisonous snake or go near the flower so it will just keep breeding and killing until somebody puts a stop to it.

Past people who have tried to kill it got bitten by the poisonous snake then fell near the plant, got bitten by that and died within 30 seconds.

In the past week the flower has killed all the members of: Busted, D12, Blue and The Darkness.

For further information call: 0800 8108 212 or visit www.killerflower.com/thesun.

Hannah Smith (12)
Redhill Comprehensive School

Bad Luck

Friday 13th March 05 - 7am
　Dear Diary,
　Hi it's about 7am and I have just woken up, it's my first day at my new school. I really *can* wait because I will get beaten up again. That's what always happens. Hang on a minute, my cat is fighting with the pen! Alright, he's gone, oh no, Mum's getting up, talk to you later.
　Love Chloe.

Friday 13th March 05 - 5pm
　Dear Diary,
　Hi my day today was alright, I have made about 5 friends, they are all really nice to me. My life seems to be getting better. Only one more problem, Mum and Dad are arguing *again*. It's always happening. Today I could hear them when I was walking home from school. I think they might split up.
　Write back later, Chloe.

Dear Diary,
　It's half an hour later and I've got to go to my auntie's house, peace and quiet at last. Probably write to you tomorrow.
　Chloe.

Saturday 14th March 05 - 1pm.
　Dear Diary,
　Sorry about the other day. I was in a rush. Anyway it's school on Monday and I can't wait. I'm all on my own in the house, Mum's gone shopping and Dad's at the pub. For once school is really good. Oh Mum's back. I'd better go and help her with the shopping.
　Chloe.

Monday 16th March 05 - 6pm.
　Dear Diary,
　I have been home from school about 2 hours and Mum and Dad have split up. I'm really upset. I have to choose who I want to live with, my mum or my dad. I don't want to upset anyone though. Who do you think I should live with? I want to live with my dad because he is really nice and gives me a lot of freedom but, on the other hand, Mum is kind too but is too protective.
　Chloe.

Friday 20th March 05 - 4pm
Dear Diary,
Mum is so depressed and Dad is so angry. Sorry I haven't written sooner but I've been at my auntie's because of the split. Guess what, I'm going into foster care. I can't cope, it would be unfair on one of them. My life is supposed to get better, not worse. I hate my life.
Love Chloe.
PS I'm probably not going to write to you anymore.

Friday 27th March 05 - 9am
Dear Diary,
My foster mum and dad are nasty. They're really horrible and are always shouting. This is the last time I'm writing.
Goodbye,
Love Chloe.
PS It was good writing to you.

Siobhan Pannell (12)
Redhill Comprehensive School

My Cat

I got my cat a couple of days ago. When we got him, he was only eight weeks old. He was only the length of a pen, he was really tiny and cute. He was a boy and his name was Kaidis but we just call him Kai. My mum always wanted to call him Harry, Alfie or Simba, but we decided to keep Kai.

He loves loads of different foods but his favourite is Whiskas. His favourite drink is water, for some reason he doesn't like milk too much.

When we got him, he was really scared and he kept running under our sofas and hiding from us all the time.

On the first day we had him, he disappeared. My mum had come home from work and he was nowhere to be seen. She rang me at school and I said that I had seen him playing in the wine rack. He had fallen down the back and was stuck somewhere behind the units. My brother-in-law, Alex, had to come round and take the front off the units to rescue him. He was underneath the freezer.

My mum blocked up the wine rack hole and now he sleeps on the top shelf of the wine rack.

His other trick is to climb up our gas fire that is like a real coal fire. We are worried he might climb up the chimney; we should probably call him Sooty!

David Saunders (12)
Redhill Comprehensive School

Cat Diary

New Year's Day

10am: Sorry I'm late but I've got a bit of a hangover. Some old git put some whisky in my milk, but let's have less of the moaning. It's a new year and I've got loads of stuff to do. See you soon.

11am: Breakfast was horrible (again). My stupid owner has been giving me sardines ever since I got here. All I can do is look longingly at the fruit bowl. Mmm, watermelon. The only good thing about coming here is being able to see Snowbell, the bushy tail, the sleek body, and best of all, the green, sparkling eyes. Well, I'll just go and have a nap. Goodbye.

2pm: That nap was lovely. I'd just woken up so I needed to get the waste out of my body. So I went out to the neighbour's garden and did my thing. I started covering it up, when suddenly a mardy woman came rushing out of the house with a fierce look in her eyes and a broom in her hands, and do you know what she did with it? She tried to hit me. I mean, they use pig poo to help roses grow, so why can't they use cats' (Cheek!)

3pm: I asked Snowbell if she'd go out with me today and she said yes. I feel like I'm on cloud 9. Result!

4pm: I've just had lunch, and for once it was nice. Guess what I had. Fine then, I'll tell you, It was sliced apple. This is turning out to be a good year.

5pm: Hmmm, let's see, oh no I've got nothing to say except I'm happy, happy, *happy!*

6pm: I'm so *happy!* Goodbye.

7pm: I've decided not to have dinner today. I want to keep a nice trim figure for Snowbell.

8pm: It turns out there's been a car crash and two teenagers have been rushed to hospital. It looks like they're going to die. Let's hope they survive.

9pm: The neighbours have told my owners that I had a poo in their garden, so I have been sent to bed early. Life's not fair. Goodnight.

11.59pm: I can't get to sleep. I still can't believe I go out with Snowbell. Well, goodbye for today then. *Yes!*

Nicholas Baxter (12)
Redhill Comprehensive School

The Swap!

'Don't ya know that you're toxic?'
'Louise, teatime,'
'Coming Mum.'

Louise was a 10-year-old girl who was mad about Britney. She had all her albums and posters. She wished she could be like Britney so much. Everything was all about to change though:

One evening Louise was watching a documentary on Britney and one of her songs came on, Louise loved that song so much. As Louise was staring at her pale ceiling, the song, 'Toxic' came into her head.

'Wakey, wakey.'
'Mum, leave me alone!'
'Britney, I'm not your mum,' said Britney Spears.

'Britney!' Louise shouted and jumped to the floor. She realised she wasn't in her room and that she really was the real Britney Spears. At first she was shocked and scared but then she liked being famous. The rest of the day she was worrying about how the real Britney was going to cope with being Louise.

It was great, singing, dancing. Everything was great until the pressure started to build. She badly wanted to be herself and be back home. The next day she decided to go back to her real home where Britney screamed, 'Change me back now!' and Louise remembered the song, 'Toxic'.

So they both sang it and a big shudder came and they were both to normal. In the end Louise didn't want to be famous anymore.

Chelsea Mitchell (12)
Redhill Comprehensive School

Gun Crime Shocks The Nation!

Today figures have been released that shocked the nation. The figures that shocked us all are that 89% of people who own guns do not have a licence. Because of that gun crime has gone up by 41%. Our new team has been out on the streets of Arnold talking to senior citizens about these astonishing figures. One woman said, 'You aren't safe anywhere, not even in your own home'.

The police have raided over 100 homes across Nottinghamshire and have seized of 1,000 firearms. Inspector Roger has told us he is appalled at the number of firearms seized over the last few months. It's even getting to the point where schoolchildren take firearms to school and threaten people with them and that is totally unacceptable. Some schools aren't bothered, they don't care about the safety of their pupils. Part of the problem is that there are too many people out on the streets begging for money. Some of them will take the money we give them and buy firearms and drugs.

If you are going to have a firearm, you must legalise it by getting a licence before you use it. To help bring down gun crime, you must not breach the rules of the licence if you do have a firearm. Nottingham is meant to be a friendly place with lots of tourist attractions.

'Crime, - let's bring it down'. The police can't do anything. You can be part of crime prevention too. If you want the UK to be a better place, you will help us to stop crime. If you're committing a crime, we're out to get you.

Matt Gell (11)
Redhill Comprehensive School

Unlucky For Some!
(An Extract)

Chapter 1

It was Friday 13th May, the unluckiest day of the year and also the night of the Year 11 prom. Everyone was running around like wild elephants getting everything ready for the big night. Year 7s and 8s were making decorations and Years 9 and 10 were practising their dance moves for the opening show of the prom.

Tomorrow there was going to be a funfair on the forest recreation ground for all Year 11s in the Nottingham area. The Year 11s were outside having the end of year photos taken of them, they were the final photos the Year 11s would be in together, they were the class of 2005. Mr Judd, the head of Year 11 was outside having photos taken too. The sun was shining and the balloons and streamers were swaying in the soft breeze, the perfect day, but now that was all to change.

Suddenly there was a massive bang, everyone froze and slowly but stiffly turned towards the school hall. Then there was a fleet of people running into the hall that was once decorated beautifully with balloons and streamers, and was now covered in red paint and smashed up. Everything was in a great heap. It turned out that the clumsiest boy in Year 7, Danny Jones, was climbing up some ladders to paint a wall, but they were a bit unstable. He fell off, the paint went flying all over the stage, he fell off into a pile of balloons and popped them all. When he had tried to stop himself from falling off the ladder, he'd pulled all the streamers down. This was supposed to be the biggest night of a Year 11's life and now a clumsy little boy had ruined it!

Nicola Gretton (12)
Redhill Comprehensive School

He's Mine
(An extract)

Michelle walked along the cold, shiny floor like she was on a catwalk. Swishing her long blonde hair about, fluttering her luscious long eyelashes, and sticking out her chest. She was wearing a short, pink frilly skirt to show off her slim legs. She walked up to her gorgeous boyfriend, Cameron. He took her soft hand and gently kissed it. Then he wrapped his strong arms around her and smelt her strawberry-scented hair as he kissed her neck. Michelle was the most popular girl in the school; she had it all, a cute boyfriend, a nice figure and popularity! She did not have a problem in the world, yet!

As the bell went, everyone went scurrying round to their classes.

'Settle down, students,' said Miss Berry in her usual posh tone, 'we have a new student whom I'd like to welcome. Say hello to Rachel Bensa!'

Just then a skinny, brown-haired girl walked into the class. Her hair was scraped back into a ponytail and she wore big, thick glasses and had train track braces on both bottom and top teeth. The girl straightened up her dungarees.

'Hi, I'm Rachel,' she snorted.

'Freak!' shouted Michelle as the whole class burst into laughter.

Rachel took no notice as she was too busy staring at Michelle's boyfriend, Cameron, who was laughing too. Her mouth dropped wide open and a little bit of drool came out the corner! Her eyes widened as she went into a daze. This daze was broken when Michelle noticed her staring and chucked a paper aeroplane at her head!

'Now class, I do not tolerate that behaviour, treat Rachel as you would like to be treated!' shouted Miss Berry.

The bell went and Michelle and Cameron went on their way to their next class. Cameron wasn't in Michelle's, he gave her a quick kiss and said goodbye! Michelle walked along the hard floor in her normal model-like way … until she saw Rachel. She strutted up to her and knocked into her with all her might. Rachel slammed into a locker so hard that it bounced her straight back off again. She then gave Michelle a look as if to say, 'What have I done?'

'Who do you think you are?' snarled Michelle.

'Wh-I-wh,'

'I saw you looking at Cameron!'

'Who? What?'

'Yeah, you know what I'm on about. Well, keep away, he's mine!' And with that Michelle walked off with a feeling of satisfaction.

After school Cameron went round to Michelle's house. She was getting dolled up to go to the cinema with him! He sat lazily on Michelle's bed and watched her as she brushed her blonde hair and carefully applied lipgloss to her soft lips. Cameron stood up and came up behind Michelle, she saw him in the mirror and turned around with a grin on her face. It was then that they shared a long, passionate kiss. Michelle closed her eyes as she went into a dreamy world, she felt like she was floating up to Heaven. Except she started falling back down when they were interrupted.

'Michelle, I thought you were going, you'll miss that film you're going to see. What's it called? 'The Ring 2' or something?' her mum called as she barged into Michelle's room.

'Mum you could have knocked,' said Michelle feeling annoyed.

Later on at the cinema, Cameron went to fetch some popcorn, he was taking ages and the film was about to start, so Michelle went to see where he was. And you'll never guess what she saw! Rachel, standing with Cameron except she wasn't wearing glasses, she had her hair down and she was wearing nice clothes. She actually looked … pretty. She seemed to be laughing about something with Cameron. Michelle wasn't having any of this. She marched up to Rachel angrily, clenched her fist, gritted her teeth, took a big swing and punched Rachel straight on the nose!

'I thought I told you he's mine!' screamed Michelle as she burst into tears of anger. Rachel, who was also in tears, fell to the floor holding her face. Michelle was about to throw another punch when Cameron pulled her away.

'Calm down babes, we were just talking!'

As Cameron went to hug her, Michelle saw something in his hand, what looked like a piece of paper. She snatched it off him and opened it up …

'Call me tonight on 9787934, lots of love, Rachel!'

After she read this, Michelle had a lump in her throat like after she'd dry swallowed a big pill, her eyes started to water!

'Just talking ay?' she blubbered to Cameron!

'We-I-we-we- were just …' Cameron tried to explain.

Michelle ran off in tears. She couldn't believe it, no one had ever done this to her before! *I've got to do something about this Rachel,* she thought! Then she realised she still had Rachel's number in her hand. She suddenly had an idea …

'I know,' she chuckled to herself, 'this Rachel freak needs telling once and for all! I have just the plan!'

'Kyle,' shouted Michelle as she walked in the door, 'would you do me a favour?'

Kyle was Michelle's big brother who would do anything for her. He came rushing down the stairs to her aid!

'Ring this number for me and pretend your name is Cameron. A girl called Rachel should answer, so say you want to meet her tomorrow after school!'

'But why?' questioned Kyle.

'Please do it - for me,' Michelle said as she fluttered her eyelashes!

'Alright, just for my little sis,' he replied.

'Thanks Bro. Say you want to meet her in Miss Berry's classroom, straight after school!'

As her brother had agreed, she ran happily up the stairs and left him to it. Michelle flung herself lazily onto her fluffy bed, and thought about her master plan. You see, Cameron wouldn't be the one meeting Rachel, Michelle would! To sort her out once and for all …

Chloe Clapp (12)
Redhill Comprehensive School

Magico's Revenge
(An extract)

It was a lovely day in the Totodile Café. The sun was beaming through the windows and there was not a cloud in the sky. The Totodiles were having loads of fun, swinging on round, steel monkey bars and throwing lovely looking pizzas down their necks. As said on the advertisements in the café, they were *the best pizzas around!* Well the totodiles certainly thought that.

The Totodiles were miniature crocodiles, about the size of a small child. They were bright blue in colour and wore nappies lined with a red-brown colour. Their vocabulary was perfect; although they spoke in a rather babyish voice.

One of the Totodiles was extremely intelligent and his name was Toto. He was slightly taller than the rest of the Totodiles, perhaps that added to the fact he was intelligent; big body, big brain. He also had an eye for another Totodile named Dilee, but hadn't got the guts to admit it.

The table Toto was sitting at was round in shape, and had quite attractive patterns carved into it. It was right by a window and Toto could feel the warmth of the sun on his back.

Toto had ordered thirty pepperoni and cheese pizzas and could see the waiter coming towards him, the pizzas stacked amazingly on his palm. Pepperoni and cheese were Toto's favourite topping and as the pizzas edged closer and closer, he could feel the drool dripping out of his abnormally large mouth and down his chin. The only thing Toto didn't know was that this was his last day eating these pizzas, in actual fact, it was his last day in the Totodile Café altogether.

'Hee, hee, hee …' A huge beast sat on his throne, staring menacingly through his crystal ball at the perfect scene of the Totodile Café. The beast was known and feared by all as Sorcero, the evil necromancer. he wore a skeleton mask to cover his ugly face, although he looked uglier with it on. The flesh and skin on his hands had been shaved off by a carving knife, leaving only the crooked bones showing. He was wearing a long, ragged leather cloak that threw a shadow over wherever it may be. Sorcero really was the definition of *evil*.

At that moment, Sorcero's disobedient servant, Magico, walked in. Magico was a fallen star on the planet, he had fallen in a great battle against Nekrom, the ruler of Hell. He was yellow in colour and always took things as a serious matter. Magico, unlike his 'master' was friendly towards the Totodiles and he knew something was going on.

'Master, what are you going to do to those poor, innocent Totodiles?' Magico questioned suspiciously.

Sorcero replied, but not exactly to answer the question, 'Silence, slave! My business is not yours!' He flew his arm out towards Magico and his pitiful servant flew across the room, landing uncomfortably in the centre of a painted circle, from which a cage erupted, towering above all else. The cage was rusted iron, though it had a magical feeling about it.

'Hee, hee, hee … now you just stay there whilst I … entertain myself.' Sorcero was boasting. He smugly turned around and walked up a flight of rotting wooden stairs. The stairs led to his casting room, the top of the tower.

Darkness fell over the Totodile Café and simultaneously, black lightning smashed through the beautiful window that Toto was sitting next to. He had to escape. The rest of the Totodiles did not think this, for they seemed to find it easier running around like headless chickens. Toto went straight for the exit, but was halted when an enormous wooden bar slammed onto the floor in front of him, blocking his path. Another window smashed, the whole place was coming down.

Chris Bridgett (11)
Redhill Comprehensive School

Death Isn't The End
(An extract)

It's starting to get dark. Early. Huh. English weather is so strange, thought Lilly as she fingered the damp moss in the dreary English autumn weather. Then, all of a sudden, she felt her long black hair being brushed into a bun.

'I hate your hair down, it spoils you.' It was her mum and Lilly was surprised because her mum didn't care about 'her mistake' as she put it. No one cared about Lilly.

'I'm going to run away,' she told her mum.

'Really? Yay! I can turn your room into a study! I'll help you pack!' said her mum excitedly.

'Oh my God. No wonder I have low self-esteem!' yelled Lilly, backing away slowly, then she started running.

Lily ran and ran, and she was half-hoping that she would hear her mum's shrill voice calling to her telling her to stop, but the eerie silence continued. After about half an hour of running, she found a forest. She took one last glance to see if her mum was trying to catch her, but all she saw were a few cars and a shop sign swaying rather creepily in the wind. Then she started walking through the forest and, after a while, she started to feel like she was being watched. She tried to shake it off but the feeling of eyes piercing into the back of her neck was still there.

'Hello?' she asked the nothingness, her voice shaking. 'Show yourself.'

Then she heard a rustle behind where she was standing. She turned around but nothing was there. She started backing towards she came from, but she tripped on a root.

'Argh!' she screamed as something … no … someone jumped on her.

'Scream all you like, no one will hear you out here,' whispered a boy, then he grabbed her hair, pulled her hair to one side and she didn't see, but she felt him bite the flesh on her neck. Blood was pouring everywhere as he held her down and drank even though she was thrashing and screaming. Then … total darkness …

Anna Wakefield (12)
Redhill Comprehensive School

Fright Night

One dark, damp, windy night Kurt, Steff and Narisha stood in fear looking at the old, broken house behind the rusty gates at the bottom of the driveway.

As one of them found the courage to open the gates, Kurt pushed them open and then fixed his short, brown, spiky hair and helped everyone into the swampy garden.

Steff (long blonde hair and green eyes) ran up to Kurt and gave him a big hug and kiss but Narisha (short, brown hair, brown eyes) thought that it was disgusting.

After that was over they crept slowly and quietly towards the house. They were scared for their lives as all three of them arrived at the stone cold door. Narisha knocked the cold door knocker. It went *bang, bang.* They all stepped back as the door slowly opened.

They entered to find ten young teenagers hanging by their necks from old, thick, dirty ropes, their faces pale blue, with cold, dark blood dripping from their necks to the floor underneath them, running towards a large, strange bookcase.

As they slowly crept towards it, *'Argh!'* They turned round to come face to face with …

Amanda Ferguson (12)
Redhill Comprehensive School

The Black Horse

'Nooooo! Why, oh why? Tell me you're joking, please!'

'I'm sorry Miss Harkins; there was nothing we could do.'

'I'll, I'll, I'll get you for this. I'll sue you I will.'

Betty was a ten-year-old stuck-up brat. She lived in South London with her parents, Nigel and Caroline. Every day Betty would go to school, not to learn but to kick up a fuss wherever possible. She would bully other kids that she was jealous of, because no one was allowed to be better than her.

Every Sunday Betty would go horse riding and it was a Sunday night when she woke up and found herself face to face with a big black horse. She tried to scream but her voice faded away into the darkness. She lay there shivering with fear, hoping, praying it would go away.

After that the black horse started appearing more often over a period of two months or so, doing strange things like stamping, bucking and jumping.

When Caroline went to collect Betty from the horse riding on the Sunday, she was told that Betty had had a tragic accident involving a black horse called *Jango*.

Bethany Peace (12)
Redhill Comprehensive School

The Robbery

The street was quiet. The headlamp which enabled drivers to see flickered on and off.

My boss released me from work, he handed me a pay cheque in an envelope. I was heading home when my phone rang. On the screen it said 'boss' so I answered it without hesitation.

'Look I know you're out of your shift but … I …'

The phone went dead. I pulled over to the side of the road trying not to block traffic. I sat in my car in horror. My boss was my friend, I didn't know what to do, but I knew I didn't have long.

I pulled my indicator down and waited to be let out of the roadside. As soon as I got out I changed to fifth gear and sped off down the road.

It was a race to get to the station. I knew I needed to get there quick. My palms were sweaty, I couldn't grasp the steering wheel. I pulled my handbrake up, took the keys out the engine and rushed up the stairs. I heard a screaming, shouting, 'Stay back or he gets it.'

I rushed to the door but it was too late. He had relied on me to save him, not to make it worse …

Narisha Lawson (12)
Redhill Comprehensive School

The Relic

'Hello, anybody there? Hello?'

Dear Diary,

This is how it all happened. I am a relic hunter and I was looking for a relic, but I had a funny feeling about it. The weather was hot and sticky and I was walking through a rainforest. I saw a piece of rope and I walked closer towards it and … *whee,* I went flying down a tunnel-type thing.

Some men said, 'I've heard something I think we have something here.'

I tiptoed through an alley. I knew I was many feet underground. The men went to the end of the big slide I'd fallen down but I wasn't there. I decided to look around for the relic, I knew it was close for I could feel it. I looked through a gap in the wall and saw the men again, they were walking away from the tunnel and they had the old pot (the relic). I had no choice but to follow them.

'Boo! 'Av got you now,' said an ugly, smelly-looking man. He had a knife to my throat.

I struggled and got away. I ran. There was the exit and the relic, I ran and …

Luke Bailey-Jones (12)
Redhill Comprehensive School

Solve One, Get One Free

I'm police officer Jackson. I've seen lots of horrible crimes but this one was the worst.

On 5th May 1993, a woman on the streets was murdered horribly, she had all her organs pulled out of her, probably by a knife. The woman was quite close to me she was … my mother.

I've been thinking about how I want to have him behind bars. I went to the crime scene and found an address book. I checked the phone book and found another murderer, who had just escaped from prison, Banes. He said he didn't do it and his fingerprints didn't match but then an anonymous caller sent a picture of Banes so he was found guilty.

Of course this was going to be an undercover job, this place was crawling with criminals, it was called the *Philadelphia Pad*.

I went in under the name of Joe Johansson. Banes didn't talk much but he said he had a twin brother who had framed him in his last murder and that his brother owned the dagger used to kill my mother. I took him in as soon as he came in. He is now in prison for the rest of his life.

Jonathan Bradley (12)
Redhill Comprehensive School

Frozen As Ice

'3 ... 2 ... 1 ... *go!*' The lifeguard shot his gun. Everyone dived off the edge into the water, gliding like dolphins then into a butterfly. I just stood there looking at my mum and Jack at the edge, their mouths were moving but no sound appeared to come out. I felt like I was a block of ice falling from the sky.

The lifeguard came up behind me and gave me a little shake, but I didn't feel it. Mum came up to me and gave me a little hug, her warmth was like a burning fire and melted me.

There was a pool of water at the bottom of me. My mum said it was from the other swimmers when they dived in but it felt to me like it was that block of ice.

My mum really wanted me to win, (all the extra money she had paid for my training) she didn't say she was upset with me but I could see it in her eyes. She whispered to me, 'It doesn't matter just wait until next year.'

Becca Haynes (12)
Redhill Comprehensive School

Watch Your Back

It started when we were coming home from our best friend's birthday party. It was pitch-black and silent then we started to hear footsteps behind us. I looked around, nobody was there so we carried on walking but then we heard heavy breathing in our ears. We were too petrified to turn around, we just ran as fast as we could. I ran and hid behind a wall. I was finally alone.

I was worried, I wondered where my friend Lilly was, I couldn't see her anywhere. She must have hidden or kept on running home. I didn't know where to go. I didn't want whatever it was to see me and get me. I did think about shouting but if the *thing* heard me I would be dead.

It was freezing and damp, I sat alone thinking of what to do. I checked in my pocket for my mobile. I must have dropped it whilst running. I could only just hear my phone ring, it must have been my mum as she would have been worried about where I was.

I heard a rustle, a scream, then silence …

Hayley Webster (11)
Redhill Comprehensive School

The Killer Story

Caz and Dez were playing a friendly game of football in the city. After about an hour they had a break.

'You want an ice cream?' asked Dez.

'Err, yes, OK, please,' Caz replied, so with that, Dez set off to the ice cream van, which luckily was only down the street.

After a long time waiting in the line, Dez returned only to find that Caz was gone! Dez continuously shouted, 'Caz!' over and over again but no luck, there was no reply to be heard. Dez was really upset but as he looked down, his luck changed as he noticed one of Caz's shoes. Dez overlooked the shoe to see a sight that made his stomach turn upside down, a trail of bloody footsteps. The blood was as red as the petals on a red rose of death. By this time Dez was panicking but nevertheless he followed them.

They led down a deep, dark alley, it was quite scary. The passage seemed to go on forever but eventually it led to the main street. When Dez noticed where he had stopped he was gobsmacked ... outside of Bloodrust Mansion.

This was the place where the police were investigating and searching for clues regarding the murders of young girls. Dez had a hunch that that was where Caz was.

The driveway was really scary but still, nevertheless, he went up the driveway. Dez pushed open the freakiest door he had ever seen in his life. He entered with caution as he did not know what was on the other side. There was a stench that lingered in the air. It was so strong that Dez could not believe he could enter this place it was really dark so Dez searched for a light switch.

'Found it!' Dez flicked the light switch to see all the kidnapped girls known to date, all dead, piled up on top of one another. It was silent, only until he heard a blood-curdling scream coming from above. It was Hannah, one of the girls that had been recently kidnapped.

'What happened to you?' questioned Dez.

With her last breath she shouted at the top of her voice, *'Gareth!'*

Gareth was a criminal from jail who the police suspected to be committing the murders. Dez looked up from Hannah to see one of Caz's shoes.

Dez's luck was changing, the shoe was at the bottom of the stairs. Dez high-tailed it to the top of the stairs to the balcony. He opened the creepy door to see Caz strapped to a chair and her mouth strapped. Dez ripped off the tape and rope. Caz gave Dez a big hug and as Dez hugged Caz, he noticed a figure, but when he blinked it was gone just like that!

Dale Cross (12)
Redhill Comprehensive School

The Girl Who Didn't Know

In the south of England there lived a grandma and her granddaughter called Rose. It was Rose's first day at Village High, she was very nervous.

She went through all her lessons with her head down and her brain in gear, she couldn't wait until after school when she could tell her gran what she'd done.

When she was on her way home she looked at the path, then looked in the sky and felt a rush of energy go through her. She stared for a moment, feeling bewildered and excited but began walking all the same. Finally she reached her cottage and burst in the door.

Her grandmother walked up to her silently and handed her a red letter. Rose looked at her gran in hesitation but opened the letter with a tear. After reading the letter she quietly said to her gran, 'I can be a witch!'

'Yes you can,' replied her gran. 'Come on we haven't got time to spare. Get your things Rose.'

They went down town and got on a train. They were going to Rose's witch and wizard school. When they arrived, Rose and her gran stood there admiring the sight of the castle.

Ten years passed and Rose became the greatest witch of all time!

Emily Head (12)
Redhill Comprehensive School

Friday The 13th: The Day Of The Dead

The wind howled hard against my bedroom window, the lightning struck angrily outside. I was sitting on my single bed with my friend Zoe.

'So, the day of the dead is when spirits from the grave come back and haunt us?' I asked curiously.

'Yeah, it happens on Friday the 13th.'

I shuddered.

All of a sudden, my door burst open. A green, slimy hand crept over the door. I gulped hard in my dry throat. Then the head of the creature appeared. It had a ripped black cloak over its head and then its legs swept around the door as fast as the speed of light.

It came closer and closer. Zoe shrieked. I got up and lifted my shaking leg and kicked it in its stomach. The creature fell back onto the blue carpet.

'Call the police!' I shouted at Zoe. She instantly grabbed the silver mobile, which lay on my desk.

The creature hurled itself up and began tugging at my leg. Zoe darted forward after putting down the phone and went to open the door.

The police grabbed the creature and explained that it was probably *The Friday the 13th creature*. I gasped and went downstairs.

Catherine Parr (12)
Redhill Comprehensive School

That Thing In The Attic

In December 2001, around Christmas time, Tom and Stephanie Smith were getting their Christmas tree ready. When Tom went up to the attic to get the tree he was in for a shock. A strange figure grabbed him and covered his mouth. He took a knife and put it to Tom's neck. He slit Tom's throat and dragged his body into the corner of the attic.

After about 10 minutes, Stephanie started to wonder where Tom was so she went up to the attic to find him but all she saw was Tom's corpse. He was dead for sure but there were no cuts or slashes on him but a puddle of blood surrounded him.

Stephanie rang up the police. When they came they knew that there was something abnormal about this murder. One of the officers rang up his friend. His friend was a psychic.

An hour later, Peter, the psychic, had arrived with some strange but hi-tech equipment. Stephanie asked him what it was.

He replied, 'It's the most sophisticated ghost tracking equipment in the world.' He went to the attic and started chanting some strange ancient ritual then he started talking to a ghost. It was the ghost that had killed Tom …

Michael Dawn (12)
Redhill Comprehensive School

The Great Escape

It was a dark, dank atmosphere within the Paris prison. I lay in the darkest, smelliest cell. I could hear the jangle of the keys in the guards' hands as they walked day after day. No one tried to escape because if they tried they would be caught, which would lead to them being shot. *Is it worth it?* I thought, *is it worth being shot?*

As I thought about whether it was worth getting shot I rememberered my son wouldn't have a father just for my foolish act. I also thought that maybe I wouldn't get caught but it was still a big risk. How could I get out? There were guards everywhere, there were enormous towers with lights and sirens on so if I did get out, the lights would catch me. There were also ID cards with fingerprint ID.

With cameras outside and inside the cells and a guard outside every cell, the only way I could get out is if something distracted the guards and the cameras but I would need an ID card and fingerprint details. If I could get a fingerprint and ID card, it would just be the cameras to distract for the great escape!

Ellis Blower (12)
Redhill Comprehensive School

The Rotting Carcass

I was in bed and the wind blew against my rickety old window. My room was black, the moonlight was shining through the window which made scary shadows. I hated my room, it was too small and had a tiny window, but worst of all the smell. It smelt like something had died under the floorboards. That was probably why my dad gave me this room. Dad said that he was the boss.

I decided that tomorrow I was going to find out what was making that revolting smell ...

At dawn I crept down the creaky staircase and outside into the tool shed. I took the rusty old crowbar out of the shed, trying not to move anything. When I was outside it was still dark and cold. I rushed back inside, closing the door behind me, then I hurried upstairs into my room, locking the door behind me. I knelt down and dug the crowbar into the boards and ripped it out; making a lot of noise.

Too much noise. My dad woke up and ran into my room, crashing through the door. He saw what I'd done. He told me it wasn't him. I looked back at the floorboards and the smell was even stronger. My eyes watered, it was a ...

Gemma Senter (12)
Redhill Comprehensive School

Ghost Kidnapper

Jane, who was a normal seventeen-year-old girl, was walking home from her mate's house on Windlow Way when *crack!*

She turned, there was no sign of anyone. Then another sound, so she started to get faster and faster until she was pulled in by something or someone.

Her mum and dad started to get worried so they rang her friend and no one had heard from her since she left her best friend's house.

Her dad went out looking for her. Her grandma rang the police while her mum was sitting still, crying her eyes out and wondering if she'd ever see her daughter again.

Meanwhile, her dad was making some progress, he'd found a piece of her clothing on a bush. Then he saw a cabin in the distance and heard screaming coming from it. It was his daughter.

The police finally arrived and they surrounded the cabin. Then her father saw a white, pale figure standing watching his daughter sitting in fear.

The police knocked the door down and the ghost disappeared. Jane's father went and hugged his daughter.

When Jane went home her mum hugged her to bits. She wondered why that had happened but knew she would never find out …

Sarah Coulson (12)
Redhill Comprehensive School

Just In Time
(An extract)

I squeezed my eyes tightly closed and rolled them up into their stalks. My life flashed before my eyes, Senika's sweet smile bored into my brain, as the one I wanted to remember for the rest of time.

I heard an ear-splitting crash and my eyes jolted open just in time to see my friend Maneala, the human, running out of the door. I peered out of the window to see the first huge crack in Pluto's huge surface with carriage 248 falling into its abyss.

'Carriage 249, calling 249, please send out emergency chains to link to carriage 247 please. I repeat, 249 connect to 247, thank you!' Maneala's voice echoed through every carriage's speaker.

I close my eyes and think back to the beginning, back to how it all started ...

'But surely mankind were intelligent enough to create a device to stop global warming,' stated Zicket, as he turned his antennae eyes towards 060.

060 said nothing but simply shook his great metal head.

Maneala sighed. 'Well, they had the power to, they were just too bothered about celebrities and taxes to go out and do it.'

'Mmm,' agreed Zicket, 'you don't mind speaking ill of your own race Maneala?'

'Yes, but Zoogs seem like such an intelligent race compared to humans,' admitted Maneala, 'they've got their priorities right.'

They turned off Moogs Row and onto Bellvyz Street. The bright sun gleamed on their faces and the lush scent of mazero flowers gently tickled their nostrils, and the gentle humming of many Zoogs created a sweet atmosphere around the three. They eventually came to a unanimous decision that Earth (before it ended one hundred and eighty thousand years ago) was nowhere near as intelligent, well-looked after and beautiful as their home, where they were now, Pluto.

The next few months dragged by but there was something different in the atmosphere, it seemed to be getting colder. And as freezing temperatures continued dropping, the three friends suspected it was more than just an early winter.

They decided to investigate this deeper. Using high power telescopes, they discovered that Pluto was moving further away from the sun and soon it would split under the pressure of an extraordinary temperature.

The sweat dripped down their foreheads, for they knew the danger was real.

'We have to do something,' croaked Maneala, her eyelashes glued together by her tears.

'We have to save ourselves,' Zicket said.

'I can't sit and watch the end of the world a second time,' decided Maneala. 'We must save everybody.'

'Bloomin' heck!' exclaimed Zicket. 'Are you suggesting we rescue the entire Zoog race?'

Maneala nodded, looking determined. They would have to save the Megisieves too, of course.

Suddenly a piece of paper flew out of 060's neck. Maneala picked it up. It read: 'So when are we going to perform this master plan?'

'Tomorrow,' Maneala said flatly.

If 060 had had eyebrows, they would have raised at that point.

'But …' Zicket began, but Maneala shushed him …

Rosa Vince (12)
Redhill Comprehensive School

Reflections
(An extract)

Have you ever met a lycha? You probably haven't, I mean, they are the rarest things in the world and the planet's biggest mystery. I have. I'll tell you my story.

It was 1939, wartime. England had warred against the Germans for two months and bombs were going off everywhere, especially where I lived, London.

It was a normal cloudy day and I was having an arithmetic test. Mrs Marks, my teacher, was pacing around the shiny, clean school room, glancing over at children's answers.

Don't come over, I thought. Too late. My light got blocked. Mrs Marks tutted, Mrs Marks nodded, Mrs Marks sighed. I could feel my ghostly pale skin suddenly turn redder than a tomato. She opened her big mouth and I prepared myself for the next rollicking but Instead of hearing my teacher's voice, I heard a shrill wail. Mrs Marks jumped, her oh-so-clean shoes squeaking as she plonked back on the ground. Madness. She flustered, ordering us around. She pushed us through the door out onto the playground and through the tin den. Then she dived in herself, sat down and straightened her hair. All we could do now was wait.

We must have been in there for about four hours. It was awful not knowing what was happening. The other girls screeched full burst for an hour. 'My nails, my hair, my clothes,' they moaned.

All I could think about was my mum.

When we were finally let out, I ran home as fast as my little legs would take me. My feet slipped on the wet pavement and my satchel banged against my leg but I didn't care. I just had this truly awful feeling that something life changing had or was, going to happen ...

Rosa Spencer-Tansley (12)
Redhill Comprehensive School

Nightmare
(An extract)

My decaying body was part of the biggest massacre since Jack the Ripper roamed free. I'll tell you about this ill-fated affair, I'll tell you how Satan dragged me to the burning showers of Hell and I'll tell you from my grave.

As I awoke in my humble home, I peered out the window to see rain falling from the heavens. I thought to myself, *another bad day* but there was truth in saying that because later on I was to die.

The wind this morning was fierce and grew louder every step I took, it was as if were trying to tell me something but I ignored it, that was the worst decision of my short life. I went to my tutor room as usual and sat down as usual, however there was something strange, there was no teacher. A message came from the speaker, it was a very jumpy headmaster, 'Children report to the school gym.' So I went, yet another bad decision. I opened the door to be greeted by ten masked men. My brown face immediately went as pale as a ghost. I almost collapsed to the floor, then it came to me I was a hostage.

I began to wonder why I was in this situation. *What have I done, I'm always good, I do my work, so why me?* I watched the frantic look on the teachers' faces. I came to the conclusion I was going to get murdered.

At ten-past twelve the men removed their masks. I noticed their ringleader, he had veiny skin and a scar running from his eye to cheek, almost like a snake, just looking at him sent a shiver down my spine.

'Stand!' The ringleader circled us like a crow stalking its prey and sniffing us, as he walked past his cruel breath could turn milk sour. 'You,' he shouted in a chilling voice. He pointed to a small boy and laughed, it was as if he were a witch with all the cackling he did. The boy took the dreaded walk to the ringleader, 'Go and stand ten yards away from me and close your eyes.' He got out his gun and pulled the trigger, the boy's body slumped to the floor in a big heap. His limp body began to stiffen. The cries of the kids grew louder as the blood from his feeble body dripped into the dark caves of death. I knew one thing, I had to get out of there …

James Mitchell (12)
Redhill Comprehensive School

The Magical Tooth

There was once a young girl called Ella, with long blonde hair and magical blue eyes. She lived with her grandma Georgina. They lived in an old rundown cottage in Wormwood Village. Everything in their cottage was very basic.

It was Ella's first day at school, she had just gone into her first lesson when she started to get a sharp pain in her mouth. It started to get worse as the day went on. She then went to the nurse at lunchtime and the nurse said she would ring home. She rang Ella's home and spoke to her grandma. She said Ella would have to come home straight away, as it was serious.

Ella finally got home after a long, painful walk, when she got back she told her grandma everything. Her grandma sighed at her, she then said to her, 'The time has come for me to tell you.' Then Ella's tooth suddenly fell out. Her grandma continued to tell and she said, 'In your life your first tooth will come out and yours just has.' She then took a long, nervous breath and then said, 'When your first tooth comes out it releases a magical power.'

Two years later Ella was at Harry Nule's Magic School. Another three years later and Ella was happily the best wizard in wizardry.

Becky Payne (11)
Redhill Comprehensive School

Camping

The night was cold and damp. Lewis was getting ready to go to bed and the time was 9.30. He was excited because the following day he was going to the woods to make camp with all his mates.

He was soon asleep in his small dinosaur quilt snug as a bug! But as he was sleeping something amazing happened. He was dreaming about the camp and it was a real success, everybody he knew was coming to his new camp because it was a secret meeting.

After the meeting all Lewis' friends were amazed at his new camp and all wanted to be in his new camp gang!

Years passed and Lewis and his friends kept their promise to keep the camp up to scratch. One day, when Lewis was 25, the camp belonged to his children, but it was demolished by bullies. So on a school holiday Lewis and a few of his mates, who used to go to the camp, helped rebuild a proper camp made of bricks and all the children loved it and kept it safe from that day forward.

Suddenly Sharon, Lewis' mum, woke him up and said it was time to go so he needed to hurry up!

Aimie Whitchurch (12)
Redhill Comprehensive School

The Great Oak

The wind was howling and screaming as I was striding through the deep, horror-stricken woods. There in front of me was the great oak. The great oak was a huge tree, its leaves were waving in the howling wind as leaves were falling off one by one. A chill of breeze arose from the sky making everything in its path cold. I stepped up to get closer, I took a few more steps then …

I woke up wondering where I was, everything around me was white, pure white. I stood up searching for an exit, in the far corner I saw a small but rather well crafted door. As I got to the door it opened, a small gnome appeared from out the bloom. The gnome was about a metre high, he had short brown hair and had a pilot hat and goggles on. I stepped through the door crouching down, banging my head on the door a few times.

I opened my eyes rubbing them again to see if it was real. The view was amazing, there were tiny mushrooms everywhere with little doors and windows in. There was also a stream flowing calmly and gently down the hill. The gnome told me he would get me out of here in no time.

I woke up wondering where I was, I was back in the woods, lying still on the floor.

Lewis Jeffries (11)
Redhill Comprehensive School

The Mystery Never Solved

It is a dark, gloomy atmosphere in Millville, and the smell of rotten apples drifts through the air. There's the sound of keys clanging against each other and it is as quiet as an ant, all you can hear is just the silence drifting through the air constantly banging against walls. Suddenly there is a sound that no one has heard ever before like a screeching type sound and everyone is awoken except one person. Everyone else is shouting, 'Let's get out of here,' and the sound is getting closer and closer.

Suddenly it just stops, everyone seems frozen to their spots, then a green light flashes over this person that has not awoken. One moment he is there, the next he has vanished. A loud piercing sound comes from up above, no one understands what is happening. A man shouts at the top of his voice, 'Wait a moment, I think that's the mayor.'

Everyone starts shouting and screaming, 'Please let him go.' It carries on taking him up to a ship that is just massive. People gasp and shout but then a screeching sound carries, all the city lights turn off, then a bang …

Atlas De Ville (11)
Redhill Comprehensive School

Suicide

The phone rang loudly, it didn't surprise me, I always get a lot of phone calls. I picked it up slowly; I didn't hear much of what he said because of the rain beating down on my windows and roof.

He said, 'I have not heard or seen my next-door neighbour in weeks, and she would have told me if she was going on holiday. Go to 7 Vyse Drive in Long Eaten, come quick.'

I slammed the phone down, got my coat on and got in my car.

I drove to the address that I was told to go; I got out my car and went into the garden. I tried opening the front door but it wouldn't move so I gave it a good kick, there was a loud bang and lots of dust seeped out of the creaky hinges but it still didn't open so I kicked it again, the door slammed open and I went in.

It smelt like the most disgusting sewer with tons of rubbish in it, it made me cough so I had to get out my tissue and cover my mouth and nose with it so I didn't breathe it in. I walked into the lounge, I looked in the chair, there was a young woman, she was in her twenties. She had been shot in her head. Her long blonde hair covered in blood made me feel sick.

The direction of the bullet came from the shattered window. I got some tweezers out of my pocket and plucked the bullet out of her head, she was facing the fireplace. I went over to the sink and washed the thick blood off the bullet. I wrote the serial number down on my note pad. I went home and searched the serial code on the Internet, it said John Jones had the murder weapon with this serial code and that his house was only two streets away from the crime scene.

I got in my car and drove to his house, I knocked on his battered door and an old man answered the door, he had grey thin hair with a bald patch in the middle and he held his walking stick tightly in one hand.

I asked him, 'Do you have a gun with this serial code?'

He grunted, 'Maybe.'

He brought out a revolver with the exact serial code apart from the last digit.

I said, 'Oh sorry for wasting your time.'

I went back to the crime scene to try and gather more evidence. I searched everywhere for more evidence. At first I thought there would be no hope, but then I looked up the chimney … there was a revolver tied on a long rubber band hanging from the top of the chimney. I had finally worked out how she had died, it was suicide. She had smashed the window to make it look like she had been shot through the window. Then she had shot herself with the revolver and the revolver would have flown straight back up the chimney so no one could find it.

'Case closed,' I said.

Harry Marshall (12)
Redhill Comprehensive School

Overboard

Why did I ever agree to come? It's so boring. All I can see for miles is water. There's just the deep blue sea, waves crashing against the ferry and the foul smell of rotten fish and saltwater.

My mum and dad thought we should have a 'holiday with a difference' this year. I was expecting them to take me to somewhere cold so we could go skiing or something, no way did I ever imagine we'd end up on a boat. Well, it is cold, but not half as fun as skiing.

I always thought when you went on a cruise, the sun was meant to be so scorching hot, you'd be dripping with sweat whilst you're sunbathing. Instead, we're all wrapped up in winter clothes, freezing to death. I wasn't expecting this at all.

The wind was blowing my hair all over the place and the rain was spitting in my face. I realised if I stayed out on top deck any longer, I would definitely catch a cold. I heaved my heavy bones down to my bedroom. I knew I would be bored stiff once I got there, but I dragged myself to my room anyway.

On my way down the corridor, I could smell the chicken dinner the cooks were cooking for tea. I sniffed again and could smell the fresh gravy and roast potatoes. At least there was something to look forward to this evening.

As I got nearer my room, I reached into my pocket and fished around for my keys. They weren't there! I checked again. They were gone! Where could they be? What could I do? I slowly walked back to the kitchen doors, searching for my keys along the way. There was no sign of them. I carried on looking, I even went back out on top deck, but I couldn't find them. It was impossible, I would never get them back. I continued to search frantically, I looked high and low, but still, they weren't there.

I looked everywhere, peering under all the wooden stools and beneath the little round tables. It wasn't easy to see anything though because a dreadful storm had begun, shaking the ferry all over the place. I checked my pockets again, just in case I hadn't looked properly last time. They were definitely not there. I wandered over to the edge of the ferry, up against the fence. I stared into the ocean, thinking of what to do. Then out of the corner of my eye, I caught a glimpse of something shiny, something silver. I turned my head slightly and looked down towards it. How could they have gotten there? I was so glad I had found them. It was my keys.

I wrapped my hands tightly around the fence, then slowly leaned forward, trying to grab them. I couldn't reach. I gripped my hands even tighter, then bent over a little further. It was really scary leaning over the side of the ferry while there was a storm. I tried so hard to get the shiny keys, but no matter how much I tried, I still couldn't reach them. I stretched out my arm even more, until I could nearly reach them. Then all of a sudden, a gigantic wave came and knocked me flying off the boat! I was absolutely terrified. Why was I ever stupid enough to lean over a boat while there was a storm?

I don't know how I got here, I just woke up the next morning and I was soaking wet, lying on the sand. I didn't know where I was, and I still don't. I've been here ever since.

Life is so dull here, I have nothing to do all day. At least the weather isn't as bad as on the ferry, but still, it's so boring on an abandoned island like this.

I have the same basic routine, from when I wake up until when I go to bed. This is my diary from yesterday:

8.30am: Woke up!
8.35am: Picked my breakfast from the fruit trees!
8.40am: Ate breakfast!
9am: Had a wash in the sea!
9.15am-12.30pm: Sunbathed and explored the island!
12.35pm: Picked fruit for lunch!
12.45pm: Ate lunch!
1.05pm-5.45pm: Swam in the sea, sunbathed and tried to relax!
5.50pm: Picked fruit for tea!
6pm: Ate tea!
9.30pm: Went to sleep in my cave.

I really wish my mum and dad would find me. I wonder if they're looking for me now. I hope so. I'm so lonely here on this deserted island, there's no one to talk to, just myself.

Every time a boat or plane passes by, I jump and wave my arms about pathetically, trying to grab their attention. They never see me though. I always fail to be seen by them. I want my mum and dad to come and take me home. I doubt it will ever happen though, but I suppose only time can tell. One thing's for sure, this certainly has been a 'holiday with a difference'!

Keila James (12)
Redhill Comprehensive School

Lone Wolf

'Quick catch them!' a deep man's voice bellowed behind me. We were being followed, more on the side of being chased. I was being carried in my mother's mouth, for I was too weak to run fast enough. She was at the front of the herd and was constantly looking for something, she must have found it for the next thing I knew I was being squished into a tight entrance to a hole. It wasn't too small, I could fit myself in it three more times with space to spin around.

I woke up the next day alone in the hole, the men had gone and from what I could tell my family and friends too. I crawled out of the hole and called for them, but there was no answer. I went back in and began to cry; I had never been on my own before, I didn't know what to do, so I explored the hole further, there was nothing there except mud and small stones.

Suddenly, I heard a whine. I knew it was too high-pitched for a wolf, but still I went out thinking maybe whoever it was could help me find my family. I stayed close to the ground in case it could beat me in a fight. It was a fox, it was a female one, her eyes were a big clue, they were huge and brown. I stared at her for a while wondering why she had cried. Then I saw it, her foot was caught in a mantrap, much like the one my sister Char had her paw stuck in once. I knew how to help her but wasn't sure whether I should help her or not. She gave another cry, which convinced me to help her. She was too weak to fight me.

I crept up to her and silently tugged her out of the trap, it had taken me around 5 minutes to have her safely out. As soon as she was out she collapsed onto the ground. I was lucky she was light and easy to carry. I decided to take her to the hole I had slept in the previous night. All the time I was carrying her there I wondered what foxes ate. When I slipped her into the hole, I went off in search of food for her and me.

Since I didn't see any healthy animals on the way I collected some berries and fruit. I found a large leaf and used it to make a parcel that my mother had shown me when I was a newborn. I took it back to the hole where I found the she fox waking up, I placed the food in-between us waiting for her to be fully awake and ready to answer questions.

'Hi, I'm Shesho, who are you?' Shesho asked dreamily.

'I'm Barse and you can eat that,' I said, noticing her eyeing the food, as soon as I said that she tucked in. This was the beginning of our adventures and friendship to find my family.

It was ten years on from my departure from my family. I was on a mission to find them. 'I think we should find some shelter for tonight and find food in the morning,' Shesho said.

'Sure and by the way have I told you how much I appreciate you coming with me and staying with me for ten years?' I asked her.

She smiled, 'Not recently, only twice every minute!' At this she gently nudged me into the little stream beside us.

Suddenly I heard a whine more specific, a *wolf's cry*! I ran as fast as I could. Shesho got the message and was hot on my heel. There was a wolf trapped in a mantrap.

'Barse, is that you? Oh please tell me you are my Barse, I have been looking for him everywhere!'

Kimberley Morley (12)
Redhill Comprehensive School

Mysteries Of The Night

He was a freakish, tall thing. Made scarier by the pitch-black of night. He had pale, clammy skin. His pupils were dilated. His arms hung limp, his head bowed to the ground. He carried an expressionless face. He looked worse than death. The bones that were supposed to occupy his legs, now popped out at obscene angles that must have undoubtedly caused excruciating pain (though he showed none). And now he was after me!

Since its cold, clammy hand had grasped me on the shoulder, I had not seen this terrifying beast. The weather had mercifully produced thick, blinding sheets of rain that protected me from catching a second glimpse.

I heard an ear-aching screech as some kind of flashy convertible came whizzing round the corner and past the next junction.

I relaxed a little and my heart slowed to a calmer rate of beats as the realisation hit me that I was nearing the city central, away from the bleak alleyways. Then I heard unnerving shuffling noises behind me. Another realisation hit me. I had forgotten to put on my glasses when leaving my flat. I cursed my forgetfulness and backed into a corner to join the darkness with all its mysteries. A sound ahead. A sound behind. Then, a croaky voice to my side, 'Eve'nin'!' Now to the other side I turned. Just as all those other realisations had hit me, so did the creature's massive, scabby hand …

Sam Geoghegan (13)
Retford Oaks High School

Paranormal Times

Stacey's Spirits - the ghosts of Stacey Manor cause an uproar.

A crowd gathered around Stacey Manor, commonly known as the Old Hall as a group of pupils found an old cellar underneath the manor, which contained old furniture from the past family who lived there. Clearly something didn't want them there so the presence tried to warn them by moving part of the furniture.

The pupils were clearly shaken up so told everyone, and that was where it all kicked off. Students started gathering in and out of the Old Hall doing Ouija boards in the classrooms to see if there were any spirits. Students started feeling cold draughts in the Old Hall and hearing things banging in the classrooms so clearly there was something in the building.

We then talked to nearby neighbours to see what they thought of the uproar.

Mr Harper had to say, 'I have never believed in ghosts and I never will'.

Mrs Walker said her grandmother used to talk about the manor and how it was haunted by the family who lived there. There was a father, a mother and daughter and one night when the father came home from the pub drunk he murdered his wife and daughter and then killed himself.

If this story is true or not we will never know but when the pupils gathered in the hall did they hear bangs and feel cold draughts or was there a natural cause for everything
concerning ghosts?

Jamie Lawrence (12)
Retford Oaks High School

The Fecrea

Amid the industrial wastelands of the modern world dwells a gruesome creature which words alone cannot fully describe. The creature is known to those few aware of its existence as the 'Fecrea'. It walks on all-fours and possesses similarities to Man. Yet no one has discovered the origin of this disgusting phenomenom, probably because all those who've ever laid eyes on it have turned and fled. Adaptation to mankind's world is how the beast survives. It feeds off waste and sewage. This leads to the nauseating stench which seeps from its every pore. The vile odour can be smelt from over a mile away although this is favourable since it usually deters anyone nearby.

The body of the Fecrea is fragile and twisted. Its skin is a sickly pale green with many repulsive blemishes. However it isn't the toxic stench, the deformed body or the revolting skin of the Fecrea that is most disturbing. Nor is it the knife-like claws or the lacerating yellow fangs. It is the dull, emotionless eyes, like tunnels of despair. The two watery marbles put those that view them into a temporary trance. In this state they are forced to behold the immense suffering that mankind has inflicted on itself and those beings around it. Wars, pollution, poverty are among the highly disturbing images that have been seen. So I warn you friend, if you ever smell something that is far too rancid to be refuse, I suggest you turn and run.

Tom Newby (14)
Retford Oaks High School

Mathematics Monster At Midnight

'Lucy are you listening? What's the square root of 49?' Miss Honey bellowed at me.

'7?'

'Lucky you knew the answer, listen next time!' she exclaimed.

Maths was boring so I decided to draw a monster although I didn't finish it.

After I had got home and finished my homework I looked at my drawing, it looked so lifeless just sitting on the page.

'I wish you were real, you could be my friend.'

'Lucy? You're not drawing again; those stupid drawings are everywhere,' my mum nagged. She'd never really liked them.

I eventually finished my monster, I was only 11 and thought it was rather good. He looked like a kind monster.

I had been in bed for hours and it had just turned midnight, I heard a rustling under my bed, I remembered the wish I had made earlier, if only it would come true!

All of a sudden from under my bed, there came a bright light ... I kept my sketchbook there and then I realised ... 'I wish he were real,' I whispered.

Pop! 'Hello, who are you?' my monster asked.

I thought it must be a dream, I closed my eyes tight and from that point on I can't remember anything. When I awoke I scrambled under my bed for my sketchbook to find that my drawing had changed, I was in it too and then my drawing disappeared and I heard a voice behind me ...

'Hello Lucy.' It was my monster!

Rebecca Newman (13)
Retford Oaks High School

Spooky Story

Paul Davies was driving home from work one very wet and windy night. Just as he was passing the local haunted castle his car started making funny noises, then it just stopped. He got quite nervous because he had heard lots of stories about the castle having ghosts and there were no buildings for miles around.

After trying to mend his car himself with no luck, feeling very cold and wet and knowing it was a long walk to the next town, he knew he was going to have to go to the castle to see if he could get help.

As the storm began to grow, he could see several dim lights in the castle as he got to a door. He knocked but nobody answered, the door just creaked very slowly open. With his heart now starting to thump and his body beginning to shake, he slowly pushed the door open and called out to see if anybody was there.

He could hear music coming from somewhere inside but he wasn't sure where from. In front of him was a very large staircase with darkly lit passages going off to the sides of it.

Should he go back outside and keep walking or face his fears inside? So he decided to go up the stairs. As he went up the stairs his heart started to beat faster because that was where the music was coming from …

Callum Harrison (12)
Retford Oaks High School

Be Warned

'Just be careful around the woods, dear. It has mysterious creatures lurking inside,' Beatrice, the new neighbour, warned. 'It even has werewolves!'

Jamie and his parents had moved to the countryside from New York.

It was incredibly stormy that night. Lightning was blazing and violent thunder crashed overhead. The piercing full moon was the only source of light between the jagged flashes of lightning. A shaggy, bear-like fir tree leant towards their dilapidated cottage and struck fiercely on the filthy windowpane looking mysteriously like a clawed hand. Jamie stepped out of his safe bed, opened the window and as he attempted to snap the branch, the sharp wind cut his face. He was being watched. Evil was overlooking him. Darkness and draughts gusted around his rigid body. Then he stopped.

To his horror, he had never heard such a spine-tingling, eerie call. A howl had just emerged from the depths of the darkness. Petrified and paralysed with fear he came to a sudden halt. What was that? Which creature had that sinister cry come from? Jamie sprinted to his parents' bedroom. Sweat ran down his face and blood pounded in his veins. Jamie burst into their room to find the duvet strewn all over the floor. He heard something behind him and turned to face it.

His eyes met with two pairs of yellow gleaming eyes glaring at him out of the black shadows. As he turned to run, suddenly the world around him was complete silence and darkness …

Sarah Chance (13)
Retford Oaks High School

That Final Second

I was strolling along from school that day. I'd had a bad day at school, I got into a fight with James McCourtny, I won of course … anyway I was strolling along when I heard something. I just kept on walking … I heard it louder.

I stopped and looked. I wish I hadn't … but you know how it feels when you hear something, you look because you don't know what's behind you. It was tall and the black outline of its body sent a shiver down my spine.

I screamed. Silence …

Maybe I shouldn't have screamed, maybe I should have run faster, maybe I shouldn't have looked. If I did then I still would be here this very day but no …

I woke up, I didn't know where I was. It was light then dark. It seemed like a petrol station. I was in a tight space, it looked to be some sort of car.

Somebody was coming, I ducked down pretending I was asleep just listening to what they would say …

They were talking about death, my death. I shivered like an animal in the North Pole, then I started sweating. I couldn't feel my feet, my teeth chattered so I shoved my fist in my mouth to stop it but it was too late, they turned around and saw me. I stared into his evil black eyes. I felt sorry for him, that second.

That final second.

Silence …

Matthew Baker (12)
The Wheldon School & Sports College

School Of Aliens

I'm telling you the truth I promise; there are aliens in the school.

It all started when Mr Clarke gave me a detention because I gave him some lip. I was there on my own because Mr Clarke went to get a cup of tea. I had just picked up a book when something tapped me. I jumped but still I turned around, no one was there. I started to shake really badly. I put the book back where I had found it, the tapping got louder as I touched this book, it was called 'Book About Aliens'. This was scary, had the book come true?

Mr Clarke still had not come back, I was getting scared, what should I do? Where should I go? I sat down, my mind racing, the lights went out. *Oh my God*, I thought, *what should I do? Help, help!* No one could hear me, there was a strange glow from under the door and the tapping was getting louder and louder. What should I do? Where should I hide? Before I could move the door flew open, I screamed as loud as I had ever screamed, closing my eyes tightly.

My body trembled as I opened my eyes again only to see a confused looking Mr Clarke. Were there really aliens in the school? I guess I will never know, but I will never forget that day and by the look on his face neither will Mr Clarke!

Hayley Johnson (12)
The Wheldon School & Sports College

Lost Key

I'm telling you from the way I saw it and the way my heart felt it. It all began on a Tuesday afternoon, me and my friend Lean were walking out of our English lesson at the end of the day. Me and Lean had to stay back with Miss Claxton for forgetting our trainers. We were walking down the corridors then suddenly it turned all quiet and no one was in sight. You could hear a pin drop. Then we saw our head teacher walking out of his office. He dropped his key on the floor behind him. The key had a label on it saying 'the key to the PE office', then Lean came up with a stupid idea. Why did I agree? Why didn't I say no?

Well I didn't so we went into the PE office and Lean opened the door. We both walked in a single file, it was like we were in dead deep trouble, you know how you get that feeling in your stomach and you feel all sick!

Lean lost her earring two days before so she was looking around and she moved the big shelf in the middle of the office and she found two buttons. She wasn't scared but I was shaking like a leaf. She pressed a random button which was the one with the arrow pointing down. A coat came down with a lift (it was a lift). I was quite relieved that it was just a lift but then I really started shaking because of the coat, we grabbed a bunch of keys in a hurry to try and get out. Lean tried all of the different kinds of keys, she got to the last one and the door opened. Lean ran out first and then I walked out. When I was walking out something grabbed my arm breathing very heavily …

Tammy Hart (11)
The Wheldon School & Sports College

Trapped

I don't know how, I don't know why, it just happened ...

Me and my mates were on a school trip to a museum, I know they are boring! It was the Natural History Museum, the place with the dinosaurs. The trip took about 2 hours, but the trip here wasn't the problem. It was that we never left the museum, you see the security system had an accident, it went haywire and it locked down ... silence.

Then the shrieks began! We were all trapped. The looks on the bones of the dinosaurs looked lifelike. We all started to wonder if we would get out of here ... I knew we wouldn't, everyone was really, really sad, the world felt like it had stopped completely. I felt shivers going right up my spine all the way to my neck, it hurt so much.

I am still in here, the air is cold, most of the class is dead including the security guard but I will not give up, I will get out. Suddenly I hear a noise, it is coming from behind me, then all of a sudden ... *bang*!

Peter Woodfine (12)
The Wheldon School & Sports College

Horror Manor

I'm going to tell it to you the way I see it. It all started from the way Tammy my best friend looked in class at school. I was curious as to what she wanted, she wanted to ask me something, I knew it but I had to be patient. After class Tammy came up to me and dragged me outside. I felt shaky, the top of my mouth was as dry as a desert. I felt stiff. I was too afraid about what she was going to say but I knew I had to be brave. As we stepped outside I shot my eyes, took a deep breath and looked at her. It wasn't until she said the words, 'Shall we go to Horror Manor tonight?' I froze and ran off.

I was in the girls' toilets when she found me, I'd been all over the school, running, hiding anywhere just so Tammy wouldn't find me. Tammy asked me why I'd ran off but I just said that I needed the toilet, luckily she believed me and we walked home.

Later that night me and Tammy went to Horror Manor and you won't believe what happened!

There was an old man standing in the doorway of the manor - 'What do you want children?' he said in a creepy voice. Tammy said we'd come to see the house but he refused to let us in. (I was relieved.)

As we walked out the pathway through the gates, Tammy pulled me into a nearby bush. (She had yet another question.) 'Shall we go round the back?' she quietly asked for the first time ever.

As she started to walk round the big, black scary manor she checked to see if anyone was watching her as she crept round the back. I slowly followed behind wondering what was going to happen. As we both walked round, it was getting scarier by the minute!

'Come on,' Tammy whispered. As we both struggled to get through the stiff door there was a big bang that ran through the house.

'I think it came from the kitchen,' I said nervously. The floorboards creaked as we slowly went across them. We heard footsteps coming from every room in the manor, it was getting louder, faster, scarier.

Suddenly there was silence. What was it? Was the house haunted? What is the legend of this scary, nasty, evil house? All these questions - no one knew the answers but there was many more to be asked!

Tammy told me to wait where I was. She went into the other room. As soon as she vanished through the door I was more scared than ever! I glared around the dark, dull room, my blood was rushing through my veins, my heart was beating faster, it was beating so fast I couldn't control myself. I had to get outside, I was the most terrified girl in the world. It wasn't until I heard Tammy scream I felt like I was in Hell!

'Aaww! My head,' I said with a great big headache. 'I must have fainted and banged my head or something.'

I squeezed through the door hoping Tammy would be behind it safe and sound, but my wish did not happen. After I went in I looked in the room Tammy went into. I saw nothing. Just for Tammy I decided to face my fears and went in to investigate, yet again I found nothing …

Emma Truman (11)
The Wheldon School & Sports College

I Should Have Said No

It all started when I slept at my friend's house. We were having a midnight feast and she asked me, 'Do you want to go and get some chocolate?'

Me being me said, 'Yes of course I will.'

When I got downstairs I heard a curious noise! I listened carefully then went towards the window, I could hear that it was coming from outside. I slowly walked towards the back door and opened it. 'Argh!' Something started to pull me down the garden path. I couldn't see anything, just feel something, my legs felt numb and I couldn't feel my hands. By this time I'd closed my eyes, I was shaking, suddenly the pulling stopped. I opened my eyes, I was in a dark, dewy, dingy room.

All of a sudden lots of light switched on and I could hear footsteps. I ran as fast as I could and came to another door. I opened it as quick as I possibly could, it creaked very loudly. I was so glad to be out of that room. I closed the door but as I turned around I got a shock - there in front of me were funny-looking creatures walking around with machines, suddenly the movement stopped, one of them had spotted me. One after another they came closer, they all joined hands and made a circle around me, my heart was pounding like a drum. They started humming, it sounded like a kind of song, I was really frightened. Then they started making strange noises, two of them let go of each other's hands and the circle split into two making two lines, one each side of me, which made a path down the middle.

Suddenly a staircase appeared, I could see one of the creatures walking down them but he was different, he was covered in jewels and had a massive gold crown on his head, I knew this one was very important. It was just trying to say something but I didn't know what, it just sounded like babbling to me and I couldn't make out a word of it.

The next thing I knew I'm sitting on a chair, I don't know how I got there. Then more and more creatures appeared and started to approach me, they started putting a rope around my body, I felt like there was a heavy weight on my chest and I couldn't breathe. I had a terrible feeling something horrible was going to happen. One by one they started walking around me in a circle. My legs still felt numb and I had developed pins and needles in my hands.

One of the creatures came right up to me and cut a strand of hair from my head and put it in some kind of liquid. Another one came towards me with a glass, there was something green in it and it smelt really bad and trust me it tasted even worse, it made me feel like I wanted to be sick, but they made me drink all of it. Why were they doing these things and what did they want?

Suddenly something very weird happened, I could understand what they were saying. One of them said to me, 'Why are you here? We want you to go away.' He kept on repeating himself again and again, he wouldn't give me time to answer. I felt weak, I knew something bad was going to happen. They untied me and made me stand up, the one in charge started to talk. They all turned to look towards him, this was my chance to escape as they had left the door open.

I ran towards the exit as fast as I could and didn't look back. Before I knew it I was back on the path, the one that had started the nightmare. In the doorway stood my friend, 'Where's our chocolate that you went to get and why are you out there?' If only she knew what had just happened.

I looked at her and said, 'The next time you ask me if I want any chocolate I think the answer will definitely be *no*!'

She just smiled at me and said, 'Come on then if you don't want any chocolate I've got the DVD ready to watch and there's lots of popcorn.'

I was only too glad to go back in the house.

Hayley Brodsky (12)
The Wheldon School & Sports College

The Creepy Room

When I went to a sleepover it all started to happen. I was just dropping off to sleep when I heard all these funny noises.

Behind me there was a room and I jumped up out of my bed and started to walk in there.

I was trembling, my fingers were shaking. I was the only one awake, everyone else was sleeping, my friends, their family were all asleep. But I was the typical one that couldn't get to sleep.

I couldn't get to sleep with all these noises, they were really scary. I went back to bed and put my quilt over my head but I could still hear these weird sounds. I put my pillow over my face and put my quilt over.

Then I could hear banging and slamming. Suddenly someone came through the door and shouted, 'Ahh! there you are.'

I had pins and needles in my hand but it was all in a dream. 'Help! Help! There's someone in here!' but nobody could hear me. I was really trembling.

Bang!

What is happening to me?

A hand grabbed my leg, I fell flat on my face, closed my eyes and was trying to shout, 'Help! Help!' but it didn't work. I was shaking more.

Help!

Lynnette Sullings (12)
The Wheldon School & Sports College

The Girl
(An extract)

I'm in school now, in my class thinking about what happened two years ago. It seemed like it happened just yesterday. I will never forget the house in the countryside!

I was right, we never should have moved here … I will tell you the story but you'll be scared and be prepared to be shocked, very shocked.

I was in the car, well the van, moving all the furniture from our old house into the big sort of mansion in the countryside. I hated it, I didn't want to move away from all my friends and family.

'Nearly there!' my mum exclaimed. I was feeling sick, sick from being squashed up in the back of the van, sick from not knowing what our new life was going to be like and sick from moving away from the closest people in my life, to a boring old village where I've got nothing and I'll be bored out my brains.

Well I'll tell you that wasn't' true. When we got to the house it was massive, much bigger than our old house. I walked in, it seemed strange and there was a large painting of a young girl on the wall, the eyes staring straight at me. It sent shivers down my back, then I just walked out of the lounge, ran upstairs and into my bedroom. Then I made it up with my wardrobes and stuff.

My mum and dad went into the garden to do some gardening to make sure it was in good condition. I was just playing in my room when I heard a noise in the room opposite me. I had never been in there because it was always locked but this time it was open …

Rebecca Glynn-Matthews (12)
The Wheldon School & Sports College

The Disappearance

Everybody knew, I mean everyone. Around this area things get out fast. I mean there was one. A murder! No not really, far, far, far worse than that ... a disappearance. No what I mean is, is that there wasn't a haunted house on a hill or anything like that involved. What I'm trying to say is that it was a normal day ... yeah ... a normal day! What I'm trying to tell you is a deadly deep secret. (Yeah right everyone knows.) But really to me it is. But anyway everyone knows different. They don't know the truth. They know something different. Not the truth. But I know the truth.

But why? Why did I know? And how did I know?

This person, this boy was a well popular, incredible, brainy mummy and daddy's boy, well-known to the area. But one *normal* day, (well this boy thought it was a normal day), he was walking alone with a book in one hand reading it and talking to someone on his mobile phone. At this time he kept hearing things. Yeah that's it ... ummm ... hearing things!

When you hear things you get really creeped out. Or maybe you think you're imagining it. Well this boy didn't, he went to check it out!

Wow! you think. I know, this boy obviously was not afraid. What he could hear was a humming sound coming from behind the bushes. As he walked he saw or shall I say imagined a dead body was hanging from a tree. Then he saw some eyes glaring straight at him, so he put himself in even more danger by looking.

I wonder what was lurking behind the bushes. Was he imagining it all?

There was a huge scream and a smash of his mobile phone falling. After that they found no dead body, no trace of the killer, no fibres or anything like that. They reckon he disappeared. *Weird,* you may be thinking. *How can you disappear?* you think.

Make sure the next time you're out alone and you hear noises it may be a killer or you even may disappear.

How do you think I know all this? Because readers ... I made that boy disappear. Shhhhhh ... !

Elishia Khan (12)
The Wheldon School & Sports College

Sweet Dreams

My head was flooding with sweat as I threw myself off a very steep hill to avoid the jaws of the beast thrashing behind me.

As I tumbled into the waters below I regretted everything I'd done that night. Why did I go into the wood? Why did I leave Jack there on his own? That was it! Beast or no beast I had to go back to save my boyfriend. Hold on, he should be the one saving me! Yeah that's right, well that's what happens in fairy tales, the prince saves Sleeping Beauty. But I am not a prince and Jack is not asleep and he's definitely not a beauty!

I pulled myself up from the stream, mud sliding through my fingers making it almost impossible to climb up. After many hours of struggling I turned around and slapped myself for my stupidity. Right next to where I'd been there were some steps.

'OK, I'm back on track, and now to the woods,' I said to myself as I conquered the last step and there he was. Jack had found me and we trotted off home. 'Yeah, right,' my story's nothing like that. Nooo I had to hike through overgrown gardens to find Jack.

And when I found him I wish I hadn't.

I knelt down beside him and whispered his name softly, 'Jack,' but there was no time to cry over my lost, crippled love. The beast was back and he sounded hungry. I hauled myself up the first tree I could find. I stared down to where my boyfriend once lay and all that was left of him was a pile of bright red steaming flesh which was being sliced up into tiny chunks and thrown into the belly of the beast. I decided it was best to stay up the tree for the night!

As I awoke I clumsily climbed out of the tree. My foot slipped sending me flying towards a muddy puddle, leaving me cold, wet and filthy. As I got to my feet I noticed a dark figure heading towards me at top speed.

It was the beast! I opened my mouth to scream, but couldn't.

'Yes it was all a dream,' I mumbled to myself as I began to wake up. As my eyes opened I saw Jack at my side and I let out a reassuring sigh. But then I saw rocks and felt a damp floor in our room. We were in a cave and at the opening there stood the beast.

And this time I could scream!

Laura Brooks (12)
The Wheldon School & Sports College

Possessed

I'm telling you this in confidence. I'm taking my chances in the hope that you won't tell another living soul, because I must tell someone. The secret is eating me away inside. The thought of it ... I can't begin to explain. You don't know what it's like living in fear of what you might do next.

You can't begin to imagine what it's like, not knowing what you do, when you do it.

It didn't start out as much. One minute I'd be doing something, then my mind would go blank. Next thing I knew I'd be doing something else.

It first occurred to be a problem when my mind was no longer blank and clenched in my hand was a knife, the sort I was forbidden to touch. Looking at the knife, there was blood dripping from it. I followed the drops to the floor, my eyes travelled across the floor to where, there lying in front of me, was my mother's lifeless body.

I could go on with an endless list of other things I did, but I'll tell you how I coped with what I had done.

I disposed of the knife in the woods by my house, under a tree with lifted roots. I ran back to the house quickly. I had to be fast even though we weren't expecting anyone and my father would be at work for hours. I couldn't be blamed for this, so the only other possible solution was to blame my dad. I ran upstairs to my parents' room, took my father's hair off his pillow and grabbed his gloves out of the drawer. I ran back down into the kitchen and took an identical knife. I smeared the knife in my mother's blood and put it at the side of her body along with my father's hair, then called the police.

My father arrived home to find the house swarming with police and forensic people. He pushed his way through the crowd, ducked under the police tape, which was isolating the house from the rest of the street. His heart thumping he searched for me and my mum until he saw the bodybag, it was then his heart sank.

He saw me standing with a police officer. He ran towards me with open arms, then when he reached me he held me so tight. Now was when the rest of my plan would follow. I couldn't become a suspect, that's why I had placed my father's hair with my mum, so I had to say this and I did. With the police officer by me, I said, 'I don't know what happened, everything was alright when you came home at lunch, wasn't it?'

The police officer hearing what I had just said took my father by the hand and said, 'Would you come this way Sir, the detectives will want to ask you some questions.'

My plan worked. I was never thought possible of killing my mum. My dad was though, in fact he was prime suspect. He even went to prison. I went to loads of foster homes, I had to leave every single one, I had to leave because I just carried on doing things I shouldn't have.

And now, I sit alone in a dark room, in the middle of nowhere. Thinking, trying to remember.

Hannah Batchford (12)
The Wheldon School & Sports College

Twisted

It all happened over 10 years ago, but I'll never forget the house on Conrick Road, number 66 haunted me then and still haunts me now! It was only me and my mum as my brother died a year before we bought the house. My mother really never got over his loss, so we didn't really bond.

But moving seemed like a good idea until I found out all the secrets, all the dread, all the horror under the basement. I could never have told Mother as she would have never believed me.

That is why I am in this room, in this hospital, she didn't believe me as I said. She thought I was mad, insane, *mental*. So she sent me here, a mental home for children. But I bet you're wondering what was under the basement. Why did she send me here? But why would you believe me as my own mother doesn't?'

But I want you to believe me, I need you to believe me when I say there was true horror under that basement. He would just sit and rock, mumbling to himself, 'Get out, evil, she's mental.'

But who was *she*?

That freaky voice was constantly going every night. It wasn't just the voice though it was the sight. The cuts, the bruises, the blood! But I chose to go down, even though I was petrified. But it was strange, this little boy looked familiar. That's why I went down there.

All the pieces were fitting together now. It was the newspaper boy, he looked like my brother. But at the start of going to hospital I wonder why my mother didn't believe me but then I knew why. That boy was down there. My mother was the insane one, she had taken him, kidnapped him.

No more excuses, I've got to come clean. It was really me. I'm the kidnapper. I beat him to a pulp. I've got the illness, split personality syndrome. That is really why I'm in this hospital. My mum never really loved me, she loved my brother and still does even though he's gone. She's the one to blame. I'll get her for it.

Georgia Binkley (12)
The Wheldon School & Sports College

He Betrayed Me

I'm telling you this because it's been eating up inside me and I need to get it out. I know the person that did it. Well of course I do, I looked quick enough. But the thing is I can't tell anyone, I want to but I can't. You must help me.

I was walking through the alley. I felt a wisp behind me, I looked but nothing was there. I felt someone's hand on my back. Then it happened, he pulled me through the bushes, tied me to a tree before he pulled the trigger. That is he looked straight into my eye almost to say, 'I'm sorry I don't want to but I've got to'. That didn't stop him, he pulled the trigger. So that's why I can't tell anyone. I can't believe it was him, the only person I could talk to, he knew all about my family. Why him? My love, my first love, my closest friend, my husband. How could he and then sit in the court pretending to smile?

Maybe one day I'll get my own back when he's sitting here in Heaven with me …

Jade Messom (11)
The Wheldon School & Sports College

The Black School

Moving here was a bad idea. It ruined everything. Everything I owned, everything I knew and every time I stepped outside, a slight flicker of fear fluttered inside of me.

I bet you're wondering what I'm talking about. I don't know how to put this. It happened a couple of years ago …

My house was small compared to the old house. This house was near a school, not an ordinary school. From the first moment I saw it, things changed.

The school looked old with old bricks, small classes, dusty windows and an overgrown lawn. Every day at 3 o'clock I'd see a few kids walking home, their faces pale with rings around their eyes. Their heads drooped and their old-fashioned bags and uniforms blowing in the wind.

On my first day at The Black School, I'd got on my favourite pair of black trousers and my favourite top. At half-past 8, Mum walked me round. The sun that had woke me up this morning at 7 o'clock had disappeared leaving a big black cloud hovering above the school. I didn't want to enter it and by the look on her face, neither did Mum.

At 9 o'clock, Mum left, leaving me, by myself, on my own, in this scary looking school. Inside was all dark, only the dusty window let in light. It was like no other school I had ever been too. There were a few students lurking around the corners, staring at me. It started thundering outside, I could see the flashing lightning. It lit the school and I could see where all of the dusty, dark rooms were.

At half-past 9 the headmistress summoned me to her office. She was old with greasy brown hair with a lot of grey strands in it. It was tied back in a rather untidy bun. She wore a long black cloak covering her black top and black skirt. The room was darker than the hall. It hadn't got any windows or lights.

The headmistress showed me around the school. I couldn't see much because of the lack of light and the dust that was everywhere. Then we came to the room 717. It looked different to all the other rooms. It was a bit lighter with cleaner but still dusty windows. The teacher looked up from her desk. She had a pale face with yellow, crooked teeth and a big bundle of hair that was all over the place. She looked awful and she smelt horrible. Her class looked pale too.

They looked like they had never had a reason to smile. It looked like somebody had painted their faces white.

As we entered, the teacher gave a weary smile, turned around and introduced herself. The class went to their desks and kept turning round and looking at me. Their eyes were bloodshot, it was very scary. I felt different here, especially now.

At 12 o'clock the bell went for lunch. I went into the bathroom to wash my hands. I looked in the mirror. Something strange was looking back at me. *No!*

It couldn't be my reflection. I was pale, like the other pupils. My eyes were bloodshot. Something was wrong. I felt my mind being drained. And then I remembered. The stormy night, the wet, slippery roads, bright headlights approaching, the screech of brakes, the smash of glass, the grinding of metal.

The scream, *my* scream.

The school was for lost souls waiting to find out the next stop of their journey, and I was there to wait my turn.

Amber Knight (12)
The Wheldon School & Sports College

The Day Of Horror

It all happened 3 years ago on the 24th August 2002, my mum was in the city centre and my dad was down at the valley working overtime. I was in the house on my own, no one else except the dog. I was sitting there watching TV when I heard a scream. It started raining and then thundering. I looked out the window and red drops were dripping. What was it? Where was it coming from?

At that very moment I heard banging from up on the roof. Then footsteps from the kitchen. Suddenly the window flew open, the footsteps were getting closer and closer. Suddenly it was silent except for the pelting of the rain on the window. Red drops were still dripping. I quickly darted upstairs to my bedroom. Just before I stepped in I heard a scream, then the thud of a body. I heard the window slam shut, I quickly dashed to the window and pulled open the curtains and let out a scream of horror, a man was hanging on rope from the gutter's pipe. A police car went past.

The next thing I knew I was in the police station getting done for 3 murders. Well 2 if you don't include the dog. As the police entered my house I was holding the murder weapon, the knife.

Now 3 years on I am serving a life sentence for murder. But to this day I can still remember the moment I picked the knife up, I saw a piece of coat on it. It looks like my ...

Nowadays when I look in the mirror I see the man dangling from the gutter. My dad came to visit me and I noticed a piece of coat was missing from his sleeve.

Tyler Lamb (11)
The Wheldon School & Sports College

November Nightmares

The night it happened was supposed to be happy and fun, but instead it was miserable and scary …

It all happened at the end of November. I was at my friend's 13th birthday sleepover and everyone was enjoying themselves. Firstly we went to the cinema and saw a scary movie, then we all had something to eat in McDonald's and finally the four of us returned to my friend's old Victorian house for the night.

Just before going to bed we had to decide who would sleep where, as there was only room for three in her bedroom. Seeing as I was the newest of the group of friends I had to be the one who slept in a different room. When I found out that I had to spend the night in the spare room, which was more like a drafty, forgotten, scary attic, I wasn't the happiest of people.

I laid my sleeping bag beside a tower of dusty cardboard boxes and slipped inside it. I thought about the scary movie we'd watched, my mum had threatened me not to watch it and told me that it would give me nightmares but I had ignored her. Now I wished I hadn't watched it. The setting of the movie was exactly the same and the characters were similar too. After about two hours of the wind whistling and the rain hammering on the small attic window, I finally fell asleep.

I was woken by a change in light. The door was ajar so I could see a faint bit of light, but now it was closed completely. I lifted myself out of my warm sleeping bag, and in the pitch-black I saw something, not a person but something, scurry across a pile of papers. Suddenly I started to hear footsteps. They didn't sound like human footsteps though. The rain was now banging loudly and fiercely on the window and the wind was so strong it made the weak wood on the roof shake. I was beginning to feel frightened. I tucked myself back into my sleeping bag and clung onto my favourite cuddly toy. The floorboards began to creak and goosebumps appeared on my arms. I was trembling so badly and fast that I couldn't stop. The strange footsteps became louder.

Everything fell silent. Then I heard heavy breathing so loud that it sounded like my own. The door handle shook and slowly and sharply opened as the tower of boxes fell on me and made me jump. A bright flicker of lightning flashed after a big roar of thunder entered through the window. I opened my mouth to scream but I was seconds too late.

Kim Watson (12)
The Wheldon School & Sports College

The Unforgettable ...

It all happened just last week. We didn't know what happened exactly, only a brief part of it, our lives will never be the same ever again.

'Let's have a sleepover,' suggested Amy.

'Yeah, let's do that at the old tree house, hey Emma,' replied Chloe.

'Yes, sleepover, okay,' said Emma as she daydreamed. They packed their bags and set off.

'I'm scared, let's turn back,' squeaked Emma.

'No, no, come on let's go before it gets dark,' replied Amy calmly.

The girls set up and started to talk when they heard a creak coming from the roof.

'What was that?' cried Emma.

'I don't know,' whispered Amy, replying to Emma's question.

'Let's try to calm down, not to worry and go to sleep,' said Chloe sympathetically. So the girls slowly lay down to sleep, but Emma was still thinking about it. That night she had a horrible nightmare. She dreamt that her two friends were kidnapped from their beds and she was surrounded by ghosts, then she awoke realising that her two friends hadn't really gone. A storm had brewed during her nightmare and hail fell down like lead stones on the roof of the tree house. She started to panic tremendously! The wind awoke the sleeping trees and startled the girls. A white figure flew frantically above them.

'What was that?' whispered Emma to Amy like she had seen a very large spider.

'I'm not so sure, but I bet this place may be haunted,' Amy replied bravely. 'Oh no more ghosts! I can't look!'

The strange white ghostly figures gathered around them. Emma saw what they were doing and she fainted, falling back into yet another deep sleep.

When she awoke, she realised that Amy and Chloe had gone. A news team got involved with the situation.

'Hi I'm Rolf Morris and I'm here today to report that two girls of the names of Chloe Morris and Amy Hook have been kidnapped. Tell me young girl, did you know these girls?' asked the reporter to Emma.

'Yes I do know them, they're my best friends. They were taken by these ghost-like things; it's really true, believe me please. Oi, get your hands off me!' Emma shouted to the reporter.

'Yes okay. Rolf Morris, Loughbough Cemetery, West Bridgford,' finished the reporter.

'I've got to find my friends. Oh where are they?' Emma mumbled to herself. Then as if from nowhere, a rustle came from beneath the leaves.

'Oh Amy, Chloe, I was so worried about you!' cried Emma in relief.

'Ay, what. What's going on?' muffled Amy and Chloe in a confused way. The news team filmed the three safe and sound inside the tree house, then the trio got back to sleep again.

When they awoke the next morning, Emma said with excitement, 'Wow, I had a weird dream about you two being kidnapped, a news team and ghosts.'

'We did too! That's very odd. How could we all have that same strange dream? Hmm!' Amy and Chloe responded to Emma trying to figure out how this could've happened to them.

'And that's how it all happened. We still don't know what really happened that night. Maybe just some weird reason but who knows what'll happen in the future?' finished Emma.

To be continued ...

Emma-Louise Wilson (12)
The Wheldon School & Sports College

Revenge Is Sweet
(An extract)

Sirens were screeching and howling all around me, they were dead, they were all dead!

It had all started 3 years ago, back then I was in the NYPD. I had a beautiful wife and a baby girl. My neighbourhood was peaceful, the sound of children playing and lawn mowers cutting the sun-drenched grass, the American dream come true. But dreams had a bad habit of going wrong when you weren't looking! I opened the door and shouted, 'Honey I'm home!' But no one answered, I repeated myself, but after that no one answered again, I started to get pretty worried. On the wall there was a 'V' sprayed on with spray paint and a syringe through the middle of it. The phone began to ring and I answered it, what happened there didn't make matters any better!

'Hello! I think someone's broken into my house and is still here, call 911!' I shouted to the person who was on the other end of the phone.

'Is this the Payne residence?' a deep female voice answered.

'Yes! Call 911!' I shouted back.

'Good, I'm afraid I can't help you,' she replied, then the phone went dead and there was silence. Then I heard a scream from upstairs.

I headed straight upstairs and there to meet me at the top was a thug, dressed in some sort of uniform. On his badge was the same 'V' with a syringe through it as the one sprayed on the wall. I got out my Berretta and aimed it at his head! 'Freeze NYPD, drop your weapons!' I shouted at the thug. Then came another scream, from my wife.

'Max! Help ... argh!' she screamed as more gunshots went off.

Without waiting for an answer from the thug I shot him and ran straight into my baby's room. Where my baby was meant to be was a knocked-over cot, inside the cot was a pool of blood and floating in that blood was my baby! I could have wept all day if my wife hadn't have been in trouble too, but she was so I couldn't wait up.

I bashed the door in and in our bedroom were 3 thugs, they all immediately started shooting at me! I took them down one by one, but I was too late! On my bed, lying there was the corpse of my wife covered in blood! 'Nooo!' I screamed as I wept over my wife's lifeless body. Everything ripped apart in a New York minute ...

Jacob Reeve (12)
The Wheldon School & Sports College

My Life Story Of Death

The day it happened was not dark and stormy like you read in horror books. That's why it surprised me. The sun was shining, the birds were singing, I was happy and did not notice it until it was too late. At first it looked like a normal face, then as I walked further, it revealed its true form. The face that I saw was terrifying, and like no other. It gradually came more and more into view, and when it did, I was chilled to the bone. The horrible person took a step towards me, and that is when I saw its horrible features. I tried to stop myself from screaming, but I couldn't, so I just ran but the person put his hand on my shoulder and as I turned round, I was frozen. I just stood there in a sort of trance, staring at the strange eyes that lay before me. I had no control over myself. I just had to follow those lulling eyes. I just walked until I came to the old, dusty warehouse.

Suddenly I was out of my trance. I tried to run but the strange eyes just pulled me back in. I was powerless to resist. The next thing I knew I was in the warehouse at knife point. What was happening? Then, a masked stranger told me to calm down, as he was only holding me hostage until someone paid for my freedom. But come on, how could I calm down? I was at knife point and probably about to die.

I just sat, treasuring the last moments of my life when I noticed he had left the room, and not taken the knife with him. I seized the chance. I quietly hooked the knife off the table, and cut the ropes that were holding me to the chair. I ran into another room, trying to find the exit, when I saw his putrid face staring, watching me, waiting for my next move. I don't know why he did it but it's all a blur to me now …

I've been dead a year now, and my killer still walks the streets, waiting for his next victim!

Ashley Dennis (12)
The Wheldon School & Sports College

The Nightmare
(An extract)

Running, running faster now than I've ever run before. I don't want to look back ever again.

I will take back these words. Once, only once to tell you the story that is now behind me. It all started on the night of spooky things, Hallowe'en. Of course ghosts, vampires all that rubbish, it's not real. Those were my thoughts as my mum told me not to go out on Hallowe'en nights.

'Tom you can go to James' house but no trick or treating,' my mum shouted, as I left the door.

Time passed, my mum had not really known what was going on. Had she? Most likely not, she thought I was going round to James' house and, well that was half right, I was meeting James at his house but not staying there. What if my mum rang? What would she do? What …

'Tom, wait up,' it was James running after me in his headless pumpkin man costume.

'Oh I must have gone past your house while daydreaming, well nightdreaming actually,' they both laughed.

'Where's it to?'

'The old barn,' I said with a shiver running down my back.

In the barn I changed to a villain who had apparently committed suicide. The costume was black and had a mask that went all the way over my head.

The hay behind us rustled.

'This place freaks me out, let's leave,' James whispered.

'What's the matter? Are you chicken?' I answered while keeping the fact that I was afraid too myself. The skies overhead were alight with lightning and clashed together by the thunder. We ran.

I can't bear the thought of what happened then. Was it a dream? No. This was real and not in my imagination. There it was, the shadow I shall now fear for the rest of my life. We turned back the way we had come. We stopped. We saw it. The trapdoor we had tripped over. Right then I could've, no would've if it hadn't been for - no, who am I kidding, I couldn't do it, I was scared. I ran past it and James stopped.

'Come on down here,' shouted James.

'No there's no time and we'd be trapped down there.' I stopped running, fear running through my veins. I was mesmerised to the spot.

'James watch out, he's …' It was too late, he'd got James. Where had he gone? I had to find out, he'd got James …

Samuel Wiser (11)
The Wheldon School & Sports College

Wake Up Call

Ella woke up to the sound of her mobile phone ringing.

'What! Who is it?' she shouted half asleep thinking it was the door bell. 'No one ever calls me at three in the mornin'!' She searched for her mobile, desperate to answer the emergency call. 'Hello?'

No one answered.

'Hello? Anyone there. If no one answers I'll hang up!'

'Wait …' an eerie voice whispered. This sent a chill down Ella's spine and her eyes widened with fear. 'If you want to live do what I tell you …'

Ella's mouth became drier with every breath she took. Grabbing the first drink she could out of the mini fridge nearby, the small mobile rang again …

'You just fell into your first challenge Ella. See, I poisoned all the drinks in that fridge and if you don't act quickly, you will die.'

'Why? Why are you doing this?'

'If you go into the kitchen I will tell you what to do and how to stop the poison.'

The kitchen was just across the hall, opposite to Ella's bedroom. Horrible thoughts ran through her head, *what if he is waiting for me outside, ready to pounce, ready to kill or what if he is lying and this is all a big prank?* Either way Ella had to find out. She tiptoed over to her door peaking through the keyhole. The door suddenly swung open, smashing into Ella's face.

'Stupid door! I've got to get it fixed!' After a brief moment of pain, Ella was back on track. She began to speak to herself, *okay I'll make a run for it.*

She put her first foot out the door and zoomed through the hall, towards the kitchen. Only just managing to stop in time.

Ella stood beside the kitchen door, preparing herself for what might happen inside. She silently slid into the dreaded room, being careful not to make a noise.

The phone rang again …

'What now? If you want to kill me, just do it!'

'On the dining table you will see three plates of food. Two of them contain a further four doses of poison that will kill you instantly and the other one contains the antidote.'

'How am I supposed to know? At least give me a clue!'

'The antidote is in the food that is best for you …'

Pork chops, pancakes and salad were laid neatly upon the table. She thought to herself, *the food that is best for you. Hmm … pork chops can't be the best for you covered in fat and the pancakes, the same. Obviously the antidote was in the salad.* Ten minutes after she had eaten all the salad, she began to feel much better, Ella had guessed right!

The phone rang again …

'Well done Ella, you aren't as dumb as you look. Your second challenge is the lounge, downstairs.'

The key to Ella's survival lay down the staircase …

She crept into the lounge and upon the coffee table were two keys. The front door and the back door keys.

The phone rang again …

'You see the keys, choose a key, one door leads to your next challenge and the other, death.'

Everywhere became silent, too silent, like the silence before murder. Ella chose the back door key. She slipped outside; there she was standing in her flooded yard, staring at a dark figure.

'Why? Why didn't I go out the front door like any other normal person would?'

The man spoke, 'No, you guessed right again Ella. Just one more task. Nearby is a thing that can kill you. If you find it you get freedom, if you don't, you die. You have thirty seconds.'

She searched for something that could kill her.

Twenty seconds …

Still no sign of anything.

Ten seconds …

She noticed something shiny, a knife, a sharp sushi knife.

'There! There! The knife!' Ella shrieked, jumping up and down.

'I'm sorry Ella, you're wrong; in the water is an electrical wire which will be activated in ten seconds.'

The man walked away as Ella's screams filled the air …

One hour later, five houses away from Ella …

'Hello, this better be an urgent situation cos I got work in the morning.'

An eerie voice began to speak, 'Listen to me closely … you have three tasks ahead of you. Do them correctly and you live, do them wrong and die …'

Holly Townsend (12)
The Wheldon School & Sports College

Animals
(An extract)

The day it happened was the best day of my life ... and the worst.

You will never understand what I am going to tell you; but I do very clearly. I believe in fate, so I'm not going to say 'if only I did this' or 'why did we do that'. It just did.

When I was sixteen I had work experience at my local zoo in Surrey. I can tell you one thing; I don't work there now.

In 2001 Mr Kyle, the manager at Surrey Zoo offered me four hours a day work experience job as an animal watcher. Animals weren't my life but I enjoyed being around them and making friends. I bet I sound like a loony, making friends with animals. Well I find them a lot easier than human friends. I think I have had one true friend all my life and I haven't been in touch with her for years. Although it's probably for the best because if she found out what almost happened she would send me to a 'home' for sure.

Mr Kyle, in the tour of the zoo, seemed a bit shifty and nervous; and when I asked to see the hen house he always changed the subject and led me somewhere else.

Now I know why he never showed me and it sends a shiver up my spine every time I think of it.

It was a sunny, cheery day and my job was getting really good. Mr Kyle was feeling generous as well. He had started giving me wages and adding a few extra pounds every week. Apparently I was doing a 'stunning job'. Well, I was feeling very proud of myself and I had finished all of my afternoon jobs, so I decided to have a wander. What a great wander it was ...

It began in the 'lions' den' then the 'bird box'. I went everywhere except the 'hen house'. Ever since I'd asked the question to Mr Kyle it had been locked up. But that day it wasn't.

I crept closer to the red wooden building and put my head against the wall trying to hear. All I could hear were noises, animal noises, but somehow they were different. Between every squawk, bark, or growl there was a word I recognised. A human word!

There must be a human in there. I took a deep breath and walked slowly and cautiously to the door, it was unlocked. I peered in but before I could focus on inside a hand touched my shoulder and pulled me back.

After that it all went dark and I can remember shouting, a lot of confusion …

Hannah Dawson (12)
The Wheldon School & Sports College

Mechanical Fault

It isn't easy, it's difficult. I mean, bringing up the subject makes my heart bleed for them. You understand when you lose someone dear to your heart, it is literally, heartbreaking. But, I have to admit it. They were great. They were my life, my happiness. They were my parents. Only, I wish this could be true. My parents were nothing but evil.

They're dead now, died on a fairground ride. It's hardly surprising, they never loved me. They loved my annoying little sister, Marie. She was their life, I was nothing. I was the 'misunderstood' one. But I hold a dark, deep secret.

I cannot begin to explain how it happened. It wasn't a long process, in fact it was very sudden. Nothing much to it. It was an accident! No a mechanical fault.

Yes. A mechanical fault.

But, don't you think it's funny that strange things always happen on normal days. Nothing out of the ordinary, just normal, happy days.

Anyway, when my parents died my sister got taken into care. She is quite happy, but I'm not and I'm not in care. I was put in a mad house with a word stamped on my hand.

'Murderer'.

Laura Cooper (12)
The Wheldon School & Sports College

Shockwave
(An extract)

Why did I go on that ride? I could have gone on another ride. I'm talking about the only stand up roller coaster at Drayton Manor Park. It's still there if you want to go and see it. Why did I go on it? I was one of those people who wanted to show everyone how brave I was, so that nobody thought I was a baby. It was a ride where it took pictures of you as you went around the track. I wish I hadn't gone on it. I bet you would have wished the same if you'd been on it. I've regretted it for the whole of my life …

It started five years ago when I was fourteen. My mum and dad took me to Drayton Manor Park for my birthday. I was really excited. When we had got our tickets I looked and stared. It was cool! It was sunny and the clear blue sky made me get a warm feeling inside me. This would be the best day of my life. I could feel it. Or would it?

I had been on twenty different rides before it was time to go home. Before long it was time that my mum said we had to leave; 4pm. I was about to leave when I froze. Even my mum and my dad froze. We stood in front of a roller coaster, staring. Suddenly Mum and Dad ran to the ride. I stood and looked. I didn't want to go on it. But I didn't want to be on my own. I had to go on. 30 seconds and that would be it! They would think I was a baby. I had no choice …

Rebecca Oakey (12)
The Wheldon School & Sports College

Waiting

I don't know whether I should be telling you this. Even thinking about it sends a cold shiver down my spine. But I need to tell you, if I don't I feel I might shrivel up with terror. It's no lie. You have to believe me. If you don't and you're ever at Whitby for some reason then visit the beach on the east side. I bet it's still there. To this day I can still remember the pure panic running through my veins, the cold wind brushing against my face, the goosebumps appearing on my skin. Listen to me! Carrying on like you know what I am talking about! But it was all so freaky, so shocking, but at the same time it all made sense to me ...

It was just a normal Friday morning. We were going on our annual weekend trip to Whitby. We had been there every year since I was two, but this time it was different. This year my dad wouldn't be there. I don't really want to talk about what happened to my dad, let's just say he's gone.

We reached Whitby at about 4pm. We went into the hotel and asked for our reserved room, but there was a problem, the hotel had been overbooked and our reserved room was full! So we decided to go to another hotel. My mum wasn't sure which hotels to try, so we finally decided it would be nice to go to a beachside hotel.

We parked in a small car park on the seafront. We went into the first hotel we saw. It was quite an old building, with tall black towers on either side, all the windows were small and thin like the type you get on old castles, the chimney was long and fat with black smoke pouring out of the top. My mum looked at me and I looked at her. She gave me a look that I had never seen before, she almost looked scared. My dad used to always look at me like that when 'they' came ...

Anyway we went into the hotel. Surprisingly they had a free room, so we took it. I ran upstairs to my room, it was right next door to my mum's. She said I had to go to sleep because we had had a long day. So I went into my room. But for some reason I didn't feel tired. I felt wide awake, like someone was with me.

Thinking my thoughts, doing what I did, I suddenly felt a rush of heat all over my body, like I was boiling over. Something was telling me to go down to the beach. So I went out my room and made my way to the beach. The owner of the hotel looked at me, I looked back at him, he was giving me that same look that my mum had given me earlier, the one that my dad used to give me when those people came to get him ... I couldn't see the people but my dad said they were there, with bright red eyes staring at him, they were the people that took him away. I missed him so much … anyway I carried on down the narrow path to the beach. I got there just before the sun went down. But believe me I would be there for a long time after the sun went down. I walked to the shore, the sea lapping onto my new trainers, but I didn't care, I still felt like someone was with me, next to me. I felt they were waiting for me. What were they waiting for? Something was messing with my mind or was it someone? Goosebumps appeared on my skin, the cold wind blew harder on my face. The sand started to blow along the beach. It was going in my eyes, I couldn't see a thing. I fell to the floor, it felt like someone had pushed me down and was holding me there. I finally got up, but as I did my right trainer came off, but I didn't notice.

I ran, I sprinted. I saw someone standing in the distance. I could see their shadow. It looked like a man. As I got closer, I realised, it was my dad. He was floating. His left hand was held out. 'I've been waiting,' he whispered deeply.

I looked into his eyes, his deep blue … no … red eyes. I took my chances, I ran, I sprinted but he just stayed in front of me, with his hand out, he kept saying something, I couldn't understand what he was saying. I actually didn't care. I was running for my life. But it wasn't helping me. There was no getting out of it. He grabbed me … and that was it.

To this day, my trainer is still there, lying, waiting.

Stacey Vizard (12)
The Wheldon School & Sports College

The Killing
(An extract)

So there I was, hearing the gunshots in the house. *Bang! Bang!* I was standing there, there in the middle of the road wondering what was happening. I'd taken a deep breath, still in horror. Who was it or who were they? I might never know! I heard the back door slam shut. I ran in terror thinking, *I'm next!*

A couple of hours later, I'd made it home. I was all alone. I was hearing the things I had heard earlier on. Sweat dripping down my face, thinking it was blood. What would you do in this situation? Wiping it from my face, I saw a dark shadow appear in front of the front door. It slowly pushed down the handle. With a great sigh of relief, I saw that it was my parents coming home early from work!

All night long, after I had gone to bed, I was just thinking about what happened. Could someone have paid the price for doing the wrong thing?

The next day, I turned the TV on and everything that was running through my head from yesterday appeared on the television in such quick time. After the news had finished, I went to my room and kept thinking, *who was in the shooting?* When I went to play out, the same things went through my mind and that I heard the gunshots again and again in the distance!

All of a sudden, I was playing football and I suddenly heard a loud gunshot going right up into the sky. I had a scent in my mind that it was the exact same man who had set the shots off in the house. Despite hearing them I carried on playing the football match. Then again the shots went off. This time they were getting even closer!

I heard rustling coming from the woods. And then, I saw a big foot come from behind the tree. I ran as quickly as I possibly could desperately trying to get away from this. As I was running, a dark, shadowed face appeared. All afraid and shocked that he had found me, I started to turn around and hide in a dark and creepy alleyway! Suddenly, little tapping noises came from the distance. The trees began to sway from side to side making it a worse experience to live for.

Slowing down and losing a lot of energy, I tore my tracksuits on a sharp nail sticking out of the wall. Blood began dripping down my weary leg, I limped as my knees had begun to stiffen up.

Turning the corner, I suddenly climbed over the wall and said out loud, 'Go away, what have I done to you?' in a calm voice.

Quickly, I fell right off the wall and on my head. I was lying there knocked out …

Ryan Campbell (12)
The Wheldon School & Sports College

Lollipop
(An extract)

Have you ever had a craving for lollipops? I have! You won't want to not after I tell you what happened to me. In fact you'll hate them, you won't be able to stand the sight of one, I can't!

I bet you're wondering what happened, I bet you think I'm just being stupid. I'm not, believe me.

I just felt happy that day. I just had the feeling you know, when you feel like doing something different. Well I didn't exactly do something different, I went shopping, alone!

I was 13, I had some independence, so I made the most of it. Anyway it was Katie's birthday today (my best friend) and I needed to get her a present. I caught the bus because my dad was being too lazy to take me. I mean aren't parents' cars supposed to be kids' taxis? Only when I got on the bus it was empty. I paid, but instead of saying that's 70p the driver said, 'Lollipop!' It sent a shiver down my spine, did I just hear right? Why would he say that? I was probably just hearing things.

I got off outside Boots, I thought there might be some nice perfume for Katie and I wanted that new nail varnish that was on telly. I walked in the shop and there I saw the bus driver, the same dark hair, the same wrinkled face and the same shiny teeth, there he was looking at the lollipops. All of a sudden he turned back and stared at me. It spooked me out so I just walked straight past him. Why was he here? Could he be following me?

Well I bought some perfume for Katie. I walked out the shop, the man was slowly walking behind me, following me I guess. I walked a little faster - so did he! I was scared, what was he playing at?

It turned out he was going to the toilet, stupid me! Anyway I ended up buying a pink box with flowers on as well. It was from Woolworths £2. I only had about £1 left and I wanted to get Katie a nice big red lollipop to go in the box, Katie's favourite and mine. So I went to the lollipop shop.

There were lots to choose from: blueberry, orange, cherry, raspberry and even a cocoa one. I looked around but I couldn't find a red one. I asked the woman if she had any left. She said they only had one left. Lucky me! I went to pay. There behind the counter was the same man on the bus and in Boots, how strange! As I put the lollipop down he said, 'Are you sure you want this one it's very big.'

'Yes I'm sure.'

'Don't do it, don't do it,' he said.
'Pardon?' I said a bit scared.
'I mean, that's 90p dear.'

As I walked out the shop I heard a voice say 'I warned you.' I hurried home because I felt really scared …

Stephanie Keating (12)
The Wheldon School & Sports College

Just A Dream
(An extract)

Now I'm going to tell you my story. It happened thirty years ago to this day. Nobody knew except me. So, this is how it happened ...

I was walking back to my house on a Monday, coming back from the shop. I had a pack of gobstoppers, you know the kind that are meant to last forever but they never do? Well anyway I got back home and saw my house door was open. I stepped inside.

Silence.

I heard a bang. My heart missed a beat. There was no sound. Not for a long, long time.

What shall I do? Where shall I go? Will I be caught? Is it just my mum or dad? All my thoughts were jumbled up. I didn't know what to do so I just stood there. Don't ask why, I know it was a stupid thing to do but that's what I did. Another bang echoed throughout the house.

Finally I decided to creep upstairs and find out who or what was in my house. The creaky floorboards moaned and groaned and for a moment I thought the intruder may have heard me. I looked out the window and what was once a wonderful sunny day was gone. It was dark. It was very dark.

Bang! Bang! Bang!

The sounds got louder. I edged to the bedroom.

Bang! Bang! Bang!

I could see a figure. Tall and dark. They were searching the room. But what for? Suddenly they edged to the door. *Where to hide?* The words were going over and over in my head. I ran into my room and jumped under my bedcovers. The figure came in. I could hear the rain lashing against the window. The figure was close to me. I could hear his breath. Louder and louder. Would they see me ... ?

Ethan Ball (12)
The Wheldon School & Sports College

The Wrong Turn

I was 12 years old when it happened, and it had thrown a shadow over my life! It all began on a chilly Friday night; I was out with my friend, Louise. We were walking the dog. We went past an old, abandoned house next to the river. It was getting dark so we decided to take a short cut through the cemetery.

We were talking and she mentioned the house by the river and she said she thought that the house was full of ghosts. I started to feel sick.

I said, 'Come on, let's hurry up and get home.'

By this time it was really dark so I grabbed on to the dog quickly. We carried on walking. Suddenly the dog just stopped for some reason. We started to hear something.

'Come to me … ha, ha, ha, ha … don't be scared … I won't hurt … together we could rule …'

We were so scared that we started to run. The dog was pulling us and then, as if someone had pushed me from behind, we fell over onto the freezing cold grass. I was almost too scared to pull up my head from its safe spot in my arms.

When I did I saw my friend lying there on the floor. I thought she was unconscious for a moment, but then I started to hear mumbling. At first I thought it was the spirit or the ghost making the sounds, but to my horror it was Louise. Someone or something was inside her, was it the spirit or something else? What would you have done? Run away? Stayed and tried to get it out of her?

I was horrified. What was it? I just lay there for a moment, staring at her! She started to say something again, I couldn't quite understand her at first but then she rolled over.

I don't know what she was, but whatever it was it was terrifying; her face was green, it was wrinkly and had many spots. She had a long nose too. I thought that she was a ghost who was a witch! I got up and so did the thing. I didn't know whether she was possessed or she was dead or anything like that! When we were both up I pushed her down so she was flat on the ground! She got back up.

I said, 'Louise?'

She answered, 'Yes?' looking puzzled. 'What's happened?'

All I could reply was, 'I don't know!'

Why did I go through the graveyard though? I could have gone the long way round! Do you believe me or was it a dream? I really don't know, but I really want to know!

Alexis Theobald (11)
The Wheldon School & Sports College

Horror In The Deep

It was something that I had dragged with me for several years. I was sorry for what I'd done. No one knows I have been screaming inside to tell someone. I have decided to tell you ...

I walked home from the late night art class at school. It was 8 o'clock and it was autumn so it got dark earlier. It walked past a large forest. Just then a pain wriggled through my head. I had fallen off my bike at a very fast speed and had a minor head injury, which caused headaches and, very rarely, hallucinations. I don't know why but I felt a force 'push' me into the forest and my legs carried me in. I knew an old man lived in a cottage a while in. I climbed through the first layer of trees. It was even darker in there than it was in a basement. A distant but close whisper made my hair stand on end.

'What are you doing here?' it wheezed.

My eyes widened and they whizzed around in my eye sockets.

'Get out!' The whisper cut through like a razor-sharp blade.

I span round and bumped into something. My eyes stared in horror at the sight that stood before me. It was an adult-sized wolf ... a werewolf. Taking a step back, my jaw hanging like a rock from a thread, I turned and ran, dodging and weaving in and out of the trees, trying to put as much space between me and the creature, presumably chasing, ripping through the trees to find me or eat me ... whatever savage werewolves do.

There was a faint structure visible through the trees. It was the old man's house! I found new strength and sprinted for the door and rapped on the solid wood. There was no answer at the door ... I pummelled it with my fist. Still no answer. I panicked. Where could an old man be at this hour? Well? Nowhere to run, so I had to fight. I snatched up a pitchfork leaning against the wall. An arm grabbed my collar. In sheer desperation I turned and rammed the pitchfork into the stomach of the wolf. I looked away as it fell with a deep groan into the murky, leafy ground. I slowly revolved my neck towards the werewolf. What I saw was impossible. It was the old man. No. It couldn't be.

I ran, ran faster than I ever had done before. I played the thoughts back. Was the man a werewolf? No. It was an hallucination. I was a murderer.

Joe Reynolds (12)
The Wheldon School & Sports College

That Night

I want to tell you but I don't, if you get me - but I'll tell you because I need to get it off my mind. It's been thirty years now. It was terrible. Friday 13th of April.

It was quiet, real quiet, so quiet that you could hear an old man waking up for his medicine. Driving along the M5 motorway on a cold, icy night, I felt the wind, cold across my face. Something was not right, someone or something was following me. My dad wasn't himself - like when they're mad and you don't dare to speak … but I spoke. It happened on that night.

Along the M5 motorway the Devil's eye crept upon me slowly. Every second, my life to live for. Icy weather sent shivers down my spine. We pulled up in an empty service station, had a bite to eat and out we came, every second felt like hours. For a split second I froze. It didn't feel right, I felt like I was taken over by an evil force.

Thud!

'What the … ?'

There he was, my dad, white face, blue lips … dead. *Bang*. Me on the floor, just a sprain. I got up.

I'm now doing life in prison for murder and I'm now paralysed in my legs …

Luke Ellis (12)
The Wheldon School & Sports College

The Soil-Encrusted Man

Strange isn't it, how children joke about them, how adults ignore them, how no one takes them seriously. But I do, because I've seen them, zombies do exist, and I can tell you exactly what happened, like the story is burnt into the back of my head.

I knocked on the door. Then ... the door started to creak slowly open. There in the doorway, framed almost impressively against the dark gloom of the hallway within, was a monster, blood dripping from its fangs.

'Trick or treat!' I yelled.

'Hi kids!' said Mrs Baker.

'Hi Mrs Baker!' I exclaimed.

'Here, have some candy, and I must say what *very* nice costumes you have there.'

'Thanks Mrs Baker!' my friend Sophie said, gratefully shoving peppermint drops into her mouth and sporting a large amount of toilet paper around her to make her look like a zombie. 'Come on Melissa, I can't wait to TP (toilet paper) Mr Kins' house, he never opens the door.'

'Bye Mrs Baker,' Sophie and I chorused.

And there it was, the old Kins' place. It had been there for centuries. No one was quite sure Mr Kins lived there anymore, but what we did know was that whenever somebody gave the ancient house a fresh new coat of toilet paper, it was clean by the next morning.

As we approached it, a bunch of boys came around a corner.

'Well, well, well, what do we have here? A couple of wittle fwirst years in rubbish cwostwumes!' said the boy, who looked like the leader of the group, in a baby voice.

The rest of the gang were doubled up with laughter.

'We have not got rubbish costumes!' I bellowed angrily, even though I knew these words weren't true because I was wearing a bunch of cat hair on every limb.

'Oh no, this one's fiery, please have mercy upon our bad, bad souls,' begged the boy.

The group jeered uncontrollably.

'I-I'm warning you, I'm a white belt in karate and I know tae kwondo!'

'Well, if you're so tough, then I *dare* you to go into the back garden of *that* house!' said the boy, now abandoning his baby voice.

I knew I couldn't back down now he had dared me. It would be against the kids' unwritten book of rules. He had trapped me.

'You're on!' I said quietly and I stepped onto the lawn of the old Kins' manor. I walked to the back gate and forced it open, and the first step I took was also my last, for out of the distance I saw something that made my heart stop.

As the first flash of lightning split the sky in two, I saw, in the distance, a rotting hand reaching out of a grave. A slimy, dirty, scabby hand was groping the air. I ran and ran. I ran past the gang of boys ... past Sophie. I just kept running, not looking back. House after house flashed past and I didn't stop until I reached my house. I slammed the door and never looked back.

I know, I know it might have been a trick of the light but I saw what I saw and nothing can change that.

Melissa Brittle (12)
The Wheldon School & Sports College

An Angel's Story

I'm going to tell you this story from inside this body, you see I'm an angel and I've taken over this body so I can tell someone my story and what happened. It all happened two years ago. I always shudder when I think of this. I can't remember everything that happened. Can I trust you with this secret? I think I can, there's just something about you, like I've known you all my life. Has anything bad ever happened to you? Well, this was much worse. I don't know why I'm telling you this, I could tell anyone, but I don't know why I've chosen you. I've just got this feeling like you're here to help and listen.

It all happened on the day when weird things happen, yeah you know, Hallowe'en. This is what happened ... me and my friends were in the park playing, joking, telling secrets, you know, but something was different, something was wrong. What really happened is serious, this sort of thing scars you for life. It happened on the day of a full moon.

Let's start from the beginning. Me and my friends, Zoey and Ruby, were at this party, but it wasn't an ordinary party, there was something different about it ... it was a Hallowe'en party. It started like this, the music was pumping, everyone was jumping and the party was happening. Then it was time for the Hallowe'en fright in the night. The lights went off and there was a long scream and a bump in the night. Suddenly a rush of cold air went through me and I shuddered with fright. The silence stabbed through me like a knife. I stood there and hesitated, knowing I was alone, all alone in an empty room, like I was lost in deep space. I felt deserted and lifeless. All of a sudden a burst of energy sprang to life inside me and I felt someone was watching me. Soon after that, a hand touched me. I went to turn around to see who it was ...

The next day at school everyone was the same but there was something wrong. No one knew what had happened the previous night.

I asked Zoey and Ruby what had happened and they both said they didn't know. This was all so weird to me then, but now I know why.

On the way home from school I felt like I was being followed, but every time I looked behind me there was no one there. I started to run, I could hear footsteps, I began to fill with fear. It was dark ...

Bang! I dropped on the floor, someone grabbed me.

When I woke up I was in the hospital, everyone was crying over some person lying in the bed. I floated over to the person, the person was dead. That person was *me!*

Sade Richards (12)
The Wheldon School & Sports College

The Beast From Within
(An extract)

He stared at me with his bloodthirsty eyes, from his very humble abode in the corner. He sat there as if waiting to pounce, unaware of his surroundings. His yellowing hook-like claws were viciously scratching at the ground beneath him. A horrific growl erupted from the beast's mouth, making me flinch. His fur was all matted with mud from the night of prowling before. Where did he come from, I hear you ask. I don't know myself, but I do know how this monstrous beast came into my possession ...

From just leaving the house of a nagging mum, I thought I deserved a treat. Nearby the school (unaware to me until just then) was a small corner shop. It looked out of place amongst all the other shops. You might one day just walk past it and not realise that it was there. As I entered the shop, a cloud of smoke escaped by the door, making it a lot easier to breathe. You couldn't see anything with the amount of smoke; it was like when it becomes foggy, but the funny thing is that it was so light and airy outside. I could just make out that the shopkeeper was an old woman. She was quiet, small and smelt of smoke. Her hair was very badly dyed a dark red colour and perched on the top of her very stubby nose was a pair of round, brass-coloured glasses.

When I looked among the shelves I could hardly see anything. Everything was completely sugar-coated in dust. I was looking for a bottle of Sprite. As I slowly approached the counter, worried I might tread on something or knock it over. I felt as though something was watching me. How could it be though? There was only me and the shopkeeper in the shop, right?

When I finally arrived at the counter after a long trek, or as I thought, the woman was gone. Suddenly something dropped. It wasn't me. I was at the counter. The shopkeeper wasn't there. There was only me. Alone. How could there be anybody else? I felt a pair of eyes fall upon me. By this time I was turned around, checking that there was no one watching me ...

Hannaa Hamdache (11)
The Wheldon School & Sports College

The Mask

Hi, my name is Danny and I want to tell you a story. I was 11 years old. I was on a chair at East Midlands airport watching all the planes coming in when I heard a noise from one of those rides where you play a joystick game. I went and put some money in, I don't know why, I just did. A dinosaur popped up on the screen, it scared me badly! Then when I realised that it wasn't real, I put my hands around the joystick and played. At the end it said *Pose For A Picture* so I did and the sign said *Ready In A Min*, so I waited. You know how when you're waiting it's like time stops still, this was one of those moments.

Pop! A photo and a certificate popped out of the side of the machine. The certificate said, 'Well done Danny,' (I'd typed my name at the beginning of the game) 'you killed 34 dinosaurs.' The photo was disgusting. It was a man with red, crinkled skin and a mask covering his face, it was so weird. I didn't want a photo like that so I chucked it in the bin.

A couple of hours later, it was our turn to get on the plane. Our seats were right at the back of the plane.

An hour later I was asleep. A jolt woke me up.

Crackle. 'This is the captain speaking, we are entering a storm. Don't be worried.' *Crackle.*

I was sitting there listening to music when another jolt, bigger, made the plane feel unstable to me. A smell, like fire, wafted everywhere. A jolt again, the plane was going down. I felt in my hand a piece of paper. The photo was back. I felt a feeling like a warning towards me, a warning from the photo.

I woke up, a pain on my leg, burning, fire. I was wedged under a seat, I fainted.

When I woke up again I was in hospital, burnt all over.

30 years on, I am red skinned and crinkled and when I look in the mirror I see … I'm not telling you because you know so there's no point, the only thing you would see is, the only thing that doesn't go with my skin is, you know what it is …

Danny Edwards (12)
The Wheldon School & Sports College

Was It True?
(An extract)

He was getting closer. I took a sharp turn left. Still he continued to follow. I could almost feel his breath blowing down my neck. He had me cornered.

Thump! I woke up at 3am, covered in sweat, hands shaking. My curtains were open and the sky was lit by the full moon. My mum came in.

'Daniel, have you had another nightmare?'

'Yeah. I think so. I mean …'

'Come on, get back to sleep.' She left the room.

You'd have thought I'd have stopped this by now. After all, I am 13. It has started to get into a routine - nightmares. I have had them ever since I was three, but this one seemed so real - as though it was going to happen.

Brrring! Brrring!

'What? Who's there?' I said drowsily.

I swung my arm out of my bed in an attempt to turn the alarm clock off, but instead it smashed on my hard wooden floor with a deafening thud. That really woke me up. I sat up abruptly and scrambled out of bed. I washed my face and went down to breakfast. Eddie, our cat, was waiting for his breakfast. I gave him his favourite - chicken. Then I prepared my own. My mum wasn't up, so I treated myself to honey on toast. It is my favourite! I went upstairs and got dressed and ready for school. My mum still wasn't up! You see, I have to get up at 6am as my school starts at 8am. I said goodbye to my mum and headed off to the bus stop. I was the first there. It was just a normal Friday. Well, so I thought …

Chloe Morris (11)
The Wheldon School & Sports College

The Woman With The White Skin
(An extract)

As I was playing my piano, my family were all upstairs getting dressed to go out. I had to stay in and house-sit. I was going to be so bored. Even my younger sister was going with them, well, I wouldn't want to babysit her, would I?

'Adam, can you please babysit your sister? She isn't coming with us, she is being naughty,' asked my mother.

'Oh, why?' I asked.

'Because I want you to,' she said.

Then I had an idea. If I looked after my younger sister, then I would earn some money. 'Okay,' I answered.

My mum and my dad were on their way out when my mum said she felt a tap on her shoulder.

'Stop tapping me,' she said.

'I'm not,' I answered.

When I closed the door, a long, slithering white thing slid over to my piano and slid inside it. I walked over to my piano and started to play it, my fingers started to shake like a leaf. My piano was out of tune. It shook the whole house.

The thing was white and it looked like a ghost! My sister ran down the stairs and she rushed to me. She said that there was a ghost in the room, so we both stayed downstairs where we both thought that we were safe, until there was a bang coming from the living room. We both held each other's hand and crept towards the room. As we approached it, we opened the door and it screeched like somebody had stood on a cat's tail. As we frighteningly took step by step, we saw an enormous brick lying there lifelessly on the tattered carpet and the window was smashed …

Tiffany Oakey (12)
The Wheldon School & Sports College

Jail

Breath ... fading. Eyes ... heavy. Hands ... bleeding. Why did I do it? I should've stayed away. I'm sure you'd do the same, wouldn't you? I know you would. If you'd heard what I'd heard and seen what I'd seen you would've probably ignored it, I should've too. Wait a minute, you don't have a clue what I'm talking about do you? Then again, I haven't even told you what's happened. Well, this is how it happened ...

There I was, walking down the street like usual when suddenly I heard a loud, high-pitched screech bombard out of the top floor of the house. Of course I wondered what it was. Usually, I would just think, *what was that?* But today was different. You see, my mum had brought me a junior detective's kit and I was feeling like the great Sherlock Holmes. So there I was, strolling up to the house, my heart pumping faster second by second. I slowly opened the door. I saw severed human body parts. My heart started to race as fast as a cheetah.

Then someone said, 'Go downstairs and make sure the door's closed.'

At that moment I felt so scared. I felt like someone had replaced my insides with a 6 tonne weight. I was just frozen. He was getting closer so I had to move, and fast! I quickly rolled behind the bin that was underneath a large drainpipe. As I heard the door close, I let out a sigh of relief. The weight had slowly gone away, but I was still scared. As I was trying to free myself, I heard the toilet flush. I looked up and suddenly a gush of blood rushed into my face. As soon as it touched me I got up and darted home.

When I got home I went upstairs and washed my hair and my face. I kept thinking about everything at that house, it made me paranoid. Every time I got wet I jumped because I thought it was blood. I just knew I had to go back ...

I slowly walked over to the house, every few steps I was having second thoughts. My thoughts were battling with myself, but before I knew it, I was there. I walked into the house knowing full well what I saw. It was quiet, a bit too quiet. As I walked into the kitchen I looked to my left to see three men staring at me. They chased me. I was so scared that day ...

So scared I got one of their knives and don't ask me why I did this, but I just felt like I had to, to get some revenge. I picked them out one by one. Bearing in mind that I was twelve …

Today I'm in jail. I've been in here for 7 years, since I was fourteen. I'd been charged with murder. by the time I get out I'll be thirty …

Jordan Bedward (12)
The Wheldon School & Sports College

The Screech!

It sends a cold shiver down my spine whenever I think about it. It is almost too unbearable to talk about, but I must tell you. If I don't tell you my mind will probably explode and you'll be the one that has to clean my brains off the floor.

I suppose it all started with that awful noise. I was with Joe and we were walking through the woods, just messing around and laughing and joking, just like we always did. We should have been starting to make our way back as it was getting dark, but I knew that if I went home my mum would nag at me and tell me to clean my room. Looking back, I wish I had gone home. It wasn't like I wanted to be there, in those woods, I didn't even like it in there, I would have preferred to have gone to the park, those woods were always a bit creepy.

Me and Joe were walking further into the wood. I wasn't scared or anything, I'm not a baby, but I have to admit I was a tiny bit creeped out, only a tiny bit, just because it was getting dark. Anyway, we came to a fork in the path, and then it began to rain before we could decide which way to go.

I spun around to ask Joe whether we should start walking home because the rain was getting worse, and I could hear thunder in the distance. 'Joe,' I said, but it was too late, he was gone. My only reply was one that I didn't want.

At first it was quiet, a low-pitch humming in the distance, but as it seemed to get closer and louder, it got higher. Soon it was an eardrum-ringing screech that went straight through me like fingernails down a blackboard. My ears were ringing with pain and the sound seemed to be draining me of all my energy.

I needed to get away from it, so I ran, I ran even though I had no idea where I was going, I ran even though it was pitch-black now and I couldn't see anything, I ran even though I might have ran into a tree at any second, I ran even though the trees seemed to be grabbing and scratching at me and even though I ran the screech was still there. It was like it was chasing me, what could I do? What would you do in that situation? I mean, I didn't even have any idea where I was, I was that lost.

I don't know how long I was running for, it could have been hours but it seemed more like days. I can remember that my legs were aching, my clothes were torn and my knees were grazed, as I had tripped over several times, but each time I had got straight back up because I was scared of what would happen if the screeching sound got too close.

My heart was racing almost as fast as I was running, and beads of sweat ran alongside raindrops down my face. I thought that I was going to pass out and then I would die alone in the woods, and no one would find me for weeks, that's if I was even still in the woods. But I didn't die, I didn't even pass out, I just kept running. I couldn't stop, my legs felt almost like they were possessed. All I could do was run, until … *Bang!*

It was the climax of the worst noise that I'd ever heard. It was so loud and high that before I had acknowledged it, I was falling towards the ground. I hit the ground with a soft thud and then there was silence. The noise stopped, I stopped, even the trees stopped. The only sound left was the sound of raindrops splashing on the ground that I was lying on. I was exhausted, I took a deep breath, I closed my eyes and fell asleep.

When I woke up in the morning, a police officer was standing over me. There was a search party out for me and Joe, but they never found him.

Jade Bullock (12)
The Wheldon School & Sports College

Him
(An extract)

Jenna was tired after her long dig at the burial site, where she was working as an archaeologist with the rest of her teammates. As she went to her tent, she thought of her bed at home and the comforts of her own flat. As she lay in her bed, Jenna thought, *just one more day until I can relax.*

As the morning came, Jenna collected a bone she was going to study more closely at her private lab in her flat.

Jenna arrived home. She threw her equipment into her lab and started to run a shower. Jenna then went into her lounge to listen to her favourite radio station. Going back to the bathroom, she realised that the voice of the presenter was not the same. She then returned to the lounge to find her favourite station. As she started to turn the tuner, she saw that the radio would not tune in. The only station that was working was channel 666.

'What is wrong with this radio?' she said.

'Nothing!'

'Who said that?' Jenna shouted.

'Me,' said the radio.

Jenna then saw the TV switch on by itself. She then saw an image of a face, a young face. Jenna screamed and ran out of the room. As she ran around the flat, she turned all of the lights on and checked every room for an invader. Her heart beat faster, she noticed she was all alone. Jenna suddenly sprinted to the front door. The lock shut.

'There's no escape, you can't get away from me,' the voice coldly said.

'No!' screamed Jenna.

'Come into the lounge now,' bellowed the voice.

'Who are you and what do you want?'

'Come into the lounge now, you fool!'

Jenna then started to walk into the lounge, peering around the door as she went. As she investigated the room, an image appeared on the TV.

It was the same face as before, but this time it was pointing straight at Jenna.

'You,' croaked the radio.

Jenna then crawled into a corner, crying. 'Please, who are you?'

'It is my turn,' replied the voice.

'What do you mean?' As Jenna looked at the image, the TV and the radio suddenly switched off.

Silence …

Gemma Rayner (12)
The Wheldon School & Sports College

The Broken Man

It was a very long time ago when it happened. I still get shivers just thinking about it. Why am I telling you? Because I feel I know you. I feel I can talk to you. It was 30 years ago. 30 years? Yes, I know, but this is something you don't forget. I was in Spain at the train station waiting for a taxi. I had three Euros left on me. I went into a shop to see what they were selling. I bought a can of Fanta Fruit Twist, a few bars of chocolate, but I still had one more Euro left on me.

I had to spend it.

Perhaps you have had that feeling? When you're on holiday and you have some money. You have to spend it. There was a scratch & win for only one Euro so I bought it. I don't know why.

I had already scratched three blocks away; two were cherries, but the other was a man - one of the ugliest men I had ever seen. He had two broken arms and legs. His neck was in a cast too. He was covered in cuts and bruises from head to toe. My blank stare got dragged away from the man's when my dad dragged me to a bright yellow taxi.

The taxi driver asked, 'Where to?'

'Airport.'

We drove for about 4 seconds until we got caught in traffic. We got out of the car and my dad said we'd walk, but the man on the card told me not to. I had no choice but to reluctantly obey my dad.

We walked down an empty part of the road. I don't know why. The path was practically deserted. Then, suddenly, the empty part of the road was no longer empty. Traffic roared through my ears as though they were driving literally in them. My dad ran to the pavement, my mum made a grab for me, but missed. Then seconds felt like minutes. A car moved towards me. Adrenaline pumping in my chest, not being able to travel to my legs. I was a deer caught in the headlights of a truck. Then a car went smack into my left hip. I flew through the air, ricocheted off another car, then landed flat in the road. Then a long, black silence.

I now still stare at the broken man but not from the card this time, no - from the mirror …

Piers Baird (11)
The Wheldon School & Sports College

The Jungle Of The Back Garden

My house has always been a bit scary. At night I'd always check the window if I heard a slight rustle in the bushes. My garden was the scariest though. It was quite big and I loved pretending I was a pirate or that I had to find the treasure before my best friend, Alice. She lived next door so we could always do loads of things. But one day, Alice was dragged shoe shopping with her mother, I was forced to adventure alone.

I saw giant trees and wild tigers before my eyes. I wasn't scared though. I'm sure you would've been. I used my trusty knife and stripped down all the towering trees and growled right back at the tigers. I suddenly heard a *l-o-u-d*, snarling voice screaming at me. It stared through the trees that I had bravely faced and I realised who this beast was. The Momster. I hurtled as fast as I could through the jungle with the Momster gaining on me from behind. The Momster went wild! Hurling the broken trees at me and with its cloak flying behind it, I had no choice but to duck for cover. With my coat shielding me from the Momster who was foaming at the mouth, I saw, from the corner of my eye, I saw a place to escape. The shedaway!

I jumped as hard as I could and landed feet first in the secret laboratory. Huge dead spiders hung above my head with broken science equipment scattered around me. I heard the Momster outside still hunting for me. I crept even further into the shedaway.

Guess what? Right before my eyes, I stumbled on a miracle. In the back of the shedaway, Professor Daddoren was trying to construct a few shelves for the Momster who owned him at the time. Most of them broke off and the Momster punished Professor Daddoren because 'men can't do anything'. I didn't understand. Anyway, on the remaining shelves, there was every single gun, bomb or whip I had ever lost to the Momster. I gingerly picked them up, my hands grabbing as many as they could. While I was smiling to myself, gloating about my discovery, the bell of Dinnerpillen rang. Dinnerpillen's the great festival of the jungle, so I dropped all my discoveries and shot up the jungle until I saw the amazing temple. I picked the lock and peeped through. Then I sat down and ate my tea before having seconds.

Grace Naghi (12)
The Wheldon School & Sports College

Baker's Dozen

It all began on that cold winter's morning. Tommy Adams was on his way to the bakers to collect his weekly loaf of bread, fresh out of the oven every morning. Just the thought of the bread made him feel warmer, well anything would on that cold morning. When he finally arrived at the bakery, it was empty, no jolly baker there to meet him with his loaf of bread, nothing. It was empty. Not even the oven had been on.

Then he got one of those feelings, you know the one where you just have to look somewhere, and this feeling was to look in the oven. Therefore, he followed his instincts and looked in the oven. He would regret this for the rest of his life ...

Sometimes I wonder why he even looked in the oven that day. The baker could have just been ill, well he could have just accepted that as an excuse, but no, he had to look in that oven on that day. Something just drew him to it.

The baker, it turned out, had been hospitalised the night before because of a fall in the house above the bakery.

Therefore, I bet you're wondering what was in that oven. You will find out as soon as I tell the tale and here it goes ...

He opened the oven gingerly. 'Holy ****!' he screamed, then he passed out.

The next time he woke up he was in an ambulance, rushing down a high street. 'Wh-what was that thing? That thing? It's there in the oven,' blurted Tommy.

'What?' asked the ambulance technician.

'That, that thing in the oven!'

'Err, Mike, he's talking rubbish, is it because of the tumour?' one ambulance technician asked the other.

'What? Hey, what tumour? I don't have a tumour!' screamed Tommy.

Then it felt as if he were gliding, he could feel the air rushing through his hair as if the roof had blown off, but in fact the roof hadn't blown off - the ambulance had gone head to head with a drunk driver. There was a sharp thud, the ambulance stopped and there was silence. The squeal of tires came next, then he couldn't hear a thing. He could see everything, but he could not hear.

Then there was a blinding light obscuring his vision. He examined the light, it felt warm, soothing. Therefore, he walked towards the light and realised that he was no longer in the ambulance, in fact he didn't even exist anymore. He was dead.

That was the nightmare he'd been having ever since he first went in that bakery. It was as if it was trying to warn him of something terrible, something terrible happening to him.

Ben Naylor (12)
The Wheldon School & Sports College

Fredrick Manor

There was nothing suspicious about the name. Fredrick Manor. An old Victorian building, in beautiful surroundings. Me, my dad, his girlfriend and my brother, Jake. We were moving there, hopefully. This was the 13th house we had viewed, the others were just not right. After my mother died, my father had taken the fussy role.

My first viewing of Fredrick Manor wasn't a good one. I was walking in the kitchen and the floorboard fell through. The second visit, a light fitting fell on my head! The third time I went to have a look by myself while my dad was talking to a strange man downstairs. I was opening the door to a small, darkened room. I stood in the middle of the room and saw a small window. Under the window was a chair, so I sat down. I turned to look out of the window and a shiver went down my spine. I turned to the door. *Bang!* A small girl stood in front of me. Who was she? Where had she come from?

'Hello,' I said.

She smiled her greeting.

I stood up and held out my hand. 'I'm Andrew.'

'Elsie,' she squealed. She must have been around 7. A curly mop of blonde hair and her huge blue eyes stood out the most.

I took a step forward and she scuttled away. It was only then that I felt my heart pounding. I wasn't scared though.

As I made my way downstairs, the strange man stared at me.

'Are you alright, love? Chosen your room yet?'

'Dad,' I said, 'did a girl live here?'

'Yes, Mr Bloomran here was just saying that a family lived here but the little girl died in a fire. She was only 7, really pretty, blue eyes, blonde hair.'

My father's words cut through me like a knife. She had seemed so real. Every time I closed my eyes she was there, looking at me.

We've been living here now for about 8 months. I'd forgotten about Elsie until I heard the noises coming from the cellar. It was a sobbing noise. Like an idiot, I went down to the cellar and she was sat there crouched in the corner. She had spikes of hair, her skin was like overcooked cheese on a pizza and her eyes were grey and dull.

'I never knew that anyone was in the house. It was me who started the fire,' Elsie confessed.

Amazing what a single match can do.

I simply closed the door and went back to bed.

Lucy Savedra (12)
The Wheldon School & Sports College

Understanding Arthur

She didn't deserve it. I didn't deserve it either ... none of us did. Do you think I was being punished? But for what? I'm babbling aren't I? Sorry. You wouldn't understand how I felt. I'll tell you what happened ...

It was a night when it looked like a cape had covered the Earth. It was silent and all was still. My mum and dad were outside, cutting down the conifers. I was sitting in the living room watching them. Have you ever had that feeling that if you stop watching someone, something really bad will happen to them? That's the feeling I had, that feeling at that very moment, as though we were being watched, as though a tiger was waiting to pounce on its prey, ready to pull its flesh from its bones.

I told myself, *Arthur, you're being stupid, sit and watch EastEnders.* So I did ...

Bang ... bang!
'Arthur!'
'Argh!'
Bang!
Silence.

I walked to the back door, breathing heavily. Sweat was trickling down my back. My hair was standing on end. All I could hear was the wind coming through the slightly opened door, my slippers on the lino and the television.

I reached for the handle ... what would I find? What would I do? Should I reach for a weapon just in case? Should I ring the police? Should I look at all? What would you do? *Snap out of it, Arthur,* I told myself.

I opened the door ...
'Argh!'
My mum and dad were lying there, lifeless. As I looked down all I saw was raw flesh in a little hole on their backs. They were being smothered in blood. Mum was closer to me. Lying there at my feet. Dead. The wind blowing through my mum's hair ... all I could do was stare.

I'm thirteen now and I'm in an orphanage. You may think I'm weird, but I made friends with a girl there called Sophie. She was lovely, bubbly, sweet and kind. She had beautiful blonde hair which was mid-length and she had green eyes and, as if she couldn't get any more beautiful, her smile was brilliant. I fell in love with her ...

Sophie always talked to me, even though she'd get the mickey taken out of her for talking to a loner.

I wanted to show her how much I loved her so when she came to visit …

I kissed her …

'Arthur, do you love me?'

'Yes,' I replied.

'I'll need some time to think,' she said, puzzled. She pecked me on the cheek and scampered out.

After two weeks we went on an abseiling trip. She still hadn't decided. I couldn't stop staring at her from the moment she started to abseil down the cliff to the time she died. How did she die? Her rope broke because they didn't secure it in the rock right, but the one thing I'll treasure always are her last words: 'Arthur, I love you!'

Carla Morris (12)
The Wheldon School & Sports College

Creepy: A Chain Of Events
(An extract)

Have you heard the story of the creeper? Well, if you haven't then here it is, but just so you know, I don't know the fine details.

It starts with a girl, you know the type. She was late going home. I don't know why or where she was coming from, she was just late. It's because of this that she had to go down Creepers Alley and as she got near the alley everything around got quiet. Just like that, there was no one on the streets of the town, no one in the shops, no cars going past. But, I'm not sure that part's true. Anyway she was home in no time at all. Then, as she got home she wondered why she had been scared of the alley. Everything was fine until she knocked on the door and there was no answer. She knocked again and again but there was still no answer. Then she pushed at the door and it was open. She went into the living room, there was no one there, then she … Well, I don't know what happened but when her parents found her she was just a heap of flesh on the floor. I bet you're wondering why I'm telling you this, well you'll have to find out for yourself, but I guess it would be quicker if I told you …

You know about superstitions don't you? Well I didn't believe in them when this story began and I didn't believe in things like witches and goblins or things that go bump in the night. And I convinced my friends not to either, it was kind of a dare. I dared them all to go down the alley. They were chickens at first, but then I said I'd go with them, that we'd do it together. Strength in numbers, we thought. Well, we were wrong, but at that moment in time they didn't know it and neither did I. It was for that reason we went down the alley.

It was easy. It was dark as we went through. The sun's warm rays were blocked by the houses on either side but as we came out into Sunny View Crescent, the sun broke through the shadows and it shone down on us. You know how when you've been in the dark for a while and then when you go back into the sun you can't see for a minute, well that's what happened to us. Only Pete (one of my friends from our group of four) kept walking, right into the road. He didn't even see it coming. Not until it hit him. He's in a coma now. I don't know if he'll ever wake up. I think I'm still in shock.

'1 down, 3 to go,' a strange voice behind me whispered …

Abigail Hart (12)
The Wheldon School & Sports College

Raw Horror
(An extract)

12/3/75 - that was when it happened, yes, I remember it like it was yesterday. What? you might be saying, so I'll tell you. I'm going to tell you what happened that dreadful day.

I was 13 and a pretty average girl; mousey-brown hair, green eyes and the usual style clothes. Anyway, it's all her fault. Why did she have to go to prison? My mum, if she hadn't got involved with drugs, Dad and me wouldn't have moved house and then ... and then it wouldn't have happened. What? you may be saying, but you are about to find out ...

It all started when Mum went away, Dad wanted me to be safe so we moved to an old Victorian house on the borders of Carlton. The house was old-fashioned with its red brickwork and black painted railings. 'Why that house?' I asked myself but that was the one that Dad wanted and he couldn't be convinced otherwise. So on the 12/3/75 we moved in. We went inside, the house looked just as old-fashioned on the inside as it was on the outside. Dad shouted at me to come and help him unpack, but I wasn't listening, I was too annoyed. I was mesmerised, it felt like the rest of the world was completely blocked out as I started to climb the stairs.

Crash! Then a pitter-patter of running of feet as if someone or something was hiding, not wanting anyone to know of their presence but made the accidental mistake of smashing something. I awoke from my trance strangely, my life flashed before me as if something was going to happen to me.

'Lucy?' Dad shouted.

I turned around speedily to see Dad's head poking cheerfully around the door. I panicked, if Dad was downstairs, who was upstairs?

My heart raced in my stomach. I gingerly climbed the rest of the stairs. I stopped, I was as scared as someone who had just seen a ghost. The room was dark and dusky, it was a dusty black cape draped over the house, only the dancing stars I could see through the window lit the dull, creepy room. If I would have known that would have been my last day living in that house or any other house I would have gone no further, but I went on ...

Amy Hook (12)
The Wheldon School & Sports College

The Man In The Mirror

I'll tell you what happened. My mum was taking me to the airport to go on holiday. But my mum doesn't really know where things are so we got a bit lost. And then, to make things even worse, the car broke down. Has that ever happened to you? Well, the only thing there was an old castle. We knocked on the enormous brown door and went in, but no one was home. There was a big mirror above the fireplace. It was a huge, rectangular mirror with a weird pattern round the edge! Why was I so interested in it? It was as if I had seen it somewhere else.

My mum looked around the castle, but I couldn't take my eyes off the mirror. My mum told me to go to bed because it was getting a bit late. I couldn't sleep, there was something wrong with that mirror, I could feel it. It was as if it was calling me, telling me to look into it.

The next morning I ran down the stairs and had my breakfast. I sat on the chair staring at the mirror. I jumped up and walked to the mirror. It was as if it were pulling me closer and closer. I started to make funny faces in it. Have you ever done that? Well, anyway, I turned around and made my hands like a gun and then span around to face the mirror again. But it wasn't me in the mirror, it was a man staring back at me. He had a long grey beard, pale, wrinkled skin and grey scruffy hair. I fell backwards when I saw him. I looked behind me but no one was there. Who was he? Why was he there? *How* was he there? Was he trying to tell me something? I was scared but those were the questions I needed to answer.

Later that day, my mum and I were watching TV. We heard a cracking noise come from the whole of the castle. It got louder and louder. Suddenly there was a big bang!

I looked up, my mum and I were on the floor outside and the man I saw had pushed us out of the castle as it fell down, he was stood by the mirror waving. The castle was just rubble. All except the mirror. It was still perfect.

That was twenty years ago when I was ten. A few months after the accident I researched the castle. I read the title of the page, it said, 'The people who lived in the castle'. I looked down the page and there was a picture of the man in the mirror. The castle had fallen down when the man and his wife were watching TV. The man saved her life just like he saved my mum's and mine. But he didn't get out. When people looked through the rubble he was nowhere to be found, but the mirror was there, not one piece of it was damaged …

The castle had been rebuilt and the same thing happened to us. But what I don't understand is why did it happen on the exact same date as it did when it happened to the man and his wife?

Emma Glossop (11)
The Wheldon School & Sports College